Business Taxes in State and Local Governments

Business Taxes in State and Local Governments

Symposium conducted by the Tax Institute of America; November 5–6, 1970

John Shannon
J.E. Luckett
F.J. Siska, Jr.
Frederick D. Stocker
John F. Due
John W. Ingram
Allen D. Manvel

George F. Break
Lee Hill
Robert F. Steadman
W. Russell Arrington
Roman S. Gribbs
Murray L. Weidenbaum
L.E. Kust

Lexington Books
D.C. Heath and Company
Lexington, Massachusetts
Toronto   London

A Tax Institute of America Publication
The purpose of the annual symposium conducted by the Tax Institute of
America (formerly Tax Institute Incorporated) is to focus attention on a
major problem of taxation by affording an opportunity for discussion by
informed participants representing different points of view. The publication of this volume carries with it, of course, no endorsement by the Institute of the views—sometimes conflicting—of the various participants.

Published simultaneously in Canada.

Printed in the United States of America.

International Standard Book Number: 0-669-81406-7

Library of Congress Catalog Card Number: 79-178851

Table of Contents

List of Tables

Foreword

I want to express one major theme that should be kept in mind as a boundary or framework for our two days together and for general appreciation of the problems of business and taxes. First of all, taxes are not an objective of government. Rather, they provide the life-blood which permits government to function. Second, the relationship between the economics of business and government is too often overlooked. They are thoroughly intermixed with the whole economy of the country. The latter, in turn, is enmeshed in all the political, sociological, and psychological problems and movements of our day. We err in not considering tax problems and their solutions as only a part of this total web of government concern and responsibility.

It has been quite a long time since the federal relationship made its major impact on business. Today, federal and state relations are adjusting with extreme rapidity to a new and more urgent set of stresses. So fluid is the situation at the moment that the future, even at modestly short range, is not easily predictable. The flow of change in our federal system does not relate solely to power and authority. It constitutes a movement toward total restructuring of the American governmental system. Business has a vital share in this evolutionary process.

Economists say all this is the result, at least mostly so, of the assault of the technological age. It also is, in part, the product of other forces. Some of these are still dimly seen, but clearly the public sphere of activity has been growing throughout the twentieth century. I think this shift of interest will continue.

In recent years, business has increasingly exercised initiative of its own in moving into the public sector on a cooperative basis. Notable examples are the voluntary efforts business leaders have exerted in minority hiring, slum rehabilitation, social programs, and pollution control.

These developments are creating stronger bonds of interdependence between business and government; and this interdependence brings with it greater complications.

It is within this framework—one of interrelated national and state concerns and goals—that the discussions of this 1970 symposium will achieve their greatest relevance and develop their maximum contemporary value.

George Kinnear

Symposium Committees

Program Committee

Chairman: GEORGE KINNEAR, Director, Washington State Department of Revenue
CHARLES B. BAYLY, JR., Columbia Broadcasting System, Inc.
LEWIS C. BELL, West Virginia University
CHARLES F. CONLON, Federation of Tax Administrators
ARTHUR M. HAYES, Standard Oil Company (N.J.)
ROBERT C. PLUMB, American Cyanamid Company
FRANK J. SISKA, JR., Sears, Roebuck and Co.
LLOYD E. SLATER, New York State Deputy Commissioner for Tax Research
FREDERICK D. STOCKER, The Ohio State University
Ex Officio:
LEONARD E. KUST, Attorney, Cadwalader, Wickersham & Taft, and President, Tax Institute of America
MABEL WALKER, Executive Director, Tax Institute of America

Committee of Hosts

Chairman: GEORGE K. DUNN, Zenith Radio Corporation
JOHN CRUNICAN, Borg-Warner Corporation
WILLIAM J. FAIT, Pullman Incorporated
GEORGE W. LUNDIN, Chicago Bridge & Iron Company
DAVID NORUM, Sears, Roebuck and Co.
JACK W. ROADMAN, Illinois Manufacturers' Association
LYNN A. STILES, Federal Reserve Bank of Chicago
WALKER WINTER, Attorney, Ross, Hardies, O'Keefe, Babcock & Parsons

Symposium Fund Committee

Chairman: R.A. GERRA, Bethlehem Steel Corporation
J.E. CARR, Norfolk & Western Railway Company
JOHN B. COOK, General Motors Corporation
B. KENNETH SANDEN, Price Waterhouse & Co.
WALKER WINTER, Attorney, Ross, Hardies, O'Keefe, Babcock & Parsons

Part I: Characteristics of a High Quality State and Local Tax System and Its Business Tax Components

I sense an air of expectancy as we are poised today to begin the 1970 symposium of the Tax Institute of America.

It is true there are many timely and appropriate topics which could have been selected for this year's program, but I believe there is none which would be of more perennial concern to a diversified, tax-oriented group such as you comprise than the subject at hand: "How Should State and Local Governments Tax Business?"

Everyone who professes knowledge on this subject has an opinion on the matter, and particularly, I think, at this moment of our history when we face on the one hand a rather restive group of taxpayers and on the other hand glaring needs in the public sector that no longer will be ignored.

Of course, it is true that all taxes are eventually borne by people, but I think this is a simplistic solution, and it is too much so to shrug off the matter of sound taxation of business in this way. Thus, the opinions and the ideas and knowledge of those in a position to know have been eagerly sought by your program committee.

In today's complex and fast-moving world, what we need even more, I believe, than foresight and hindsight, is insight. I am confident that we will see evidence of such insight today beginning with the extremely qualified speakers for this morning's session.

Certainly by the time we have heard from a representative of the Advisory Commission on Intergovernmental Relations, from a state tax administrator, from a tax specialist representing the business world, and from an economist, I think we should have much better insights concerning the characteristics of a high quality state and local tax system and its business tax components.

It appears to me that as industry is eagerly courted and rather aggressively sought by so many state and local governments, it is vitally important that industry be taxed equitably.

I believe it is equally important that such an economic group support an adequate and fair share—and I would put quotes around "fair share" because this means different things to different people—but it is important that business should support its fair share of the added burden of a high quality public sector set of facilities, which they not only make possible, but which industry has also come to expect as the price for moving into a community, or for that matter, simply remaining in a given location and expanding there.

Let's hope we are moving in that double-barreled direction. As Oliver Wendell Holmes is credited with saying, "The great thing in this world is not so much where we are going, but in what direction we are going."

Lewis C. Bell
Professor of Economics, West Virginia University, and Chairman of Thursday Morning Session

1 Characteristics of a High Quality State and Local Tax System

John Shannon

Anyone who sets out to tell state and local policymakers how they should go about constructing a high quality tax system must possess two attributes in abundance. First, he must exhibit an unquestioned willingness to instruct others in their duty. Second, he must inspire the type of confidence that prompts people to say, "He may be wrong, but he's never in doubt!"

With these apologies out of the way I shall now attempt to answer three questions:

1. What are the essential characteristics of a high quality state-local revenue system?
2. What is the basic rationale that underpins these high quality characteristics?
3. What are the implications of a high quality state-local revenue system for the business community?

Before dealing with these issues it should be made clear that the views expressed are primarily those enunciated by the Advisory Commission on Intergovernmental Relations over the last ten years. Our bipartisan Commission was created by Congress in 1959 and it is composed of 26 representatives from all levels of government and the general public. Senator Russell Arrington of Illinois, who will be one of our symposium speakers, is a member of the Commission.

The basic goal of the Commission is to strengthen our federal system of government by supporting policies designed primarily to bolster the weaker partners—state and local governments. The Commission's proposals for developing a more productive and equitable state-local revenue system, therefore, must be viewed as one financial means to accomplish a political end—that of strengthening our decentralized system of government.

Essential Characteristics and Rationale of a High Quality Tax System

In my judgment it is possible to distill from the eleven Commission reports on this subject,[1] four essential characteristics of a productive and equitable state-local revenue system:

3

1. State use of both a personal income tax and a general retail sales levy.
2. A set of state policies designed to insure a fairly high degree of property tax assessment uniformity.
3. State action that can effectively shield low-income households from excessive sales and property tax burdens.
4. A tough state policy to govern local use of income and sales taxes.

State Use of Personal Income and Sales Tax

There is increased support for the idea that a state must make use of both revenue workhorses—the general retail sales tax and the personal income tax. It is true that there is still some heavy political sniping going on between the champions of the personal income tax on the one hand and the sales tax on the other. Nevertheless, it is becoming increasingly apparent that the demands of taxpayer equity, revenue productivity, and the need to stay competitive will force more and more states to hitch their revenue wagons to heavy-duty income and sales tax horses. The perennial sales versus income tax debate is becoming a luxury that few states can afford—they need both.

Thirty-three states now levy both personal income and retail sales taxes. Even more significant is the fact that fourteen states have joined the "double tax" ranks since 1960.

Tax Equity Issue. On the tax equity, or tax distribution, side there is also greater agreement. The mobility of high-income persons and capital and the growing state concern for economic development suggest that the task of income redistribution by means of steeply progressive taxes must be left to the national government with its superior jurisdictional reach.

If limited jurisdiction forecloses the adoption of highly progressive tax policies, the states' growing reliance on consumer taxes places severe limitations on the use of regressive tax policies. To put the issue more bluntly, can a sales tax collector take more than $1 for every $20 of food purchases? Here again we see a growing body of public opinion that favors either the outright exemption of food or some system of tax credits and cash refunds to pull the regressive stinger from the retail sales tax.

By the same token, states have demonstrated that the sales tax need not be severely regressive—that either the exemption of food or appropriate tax credits can transform this tax into a proportional levy for the great mass of taxpayers. At the present time sixteen states exempt food outright while six states (Indiana, Colorado, Hawaii, Massachusetts, Vermont, and Nebraska) permit state income taxpayers to credit their sales tax payments against the personal income tax.

These recent and pioneering tax credit and refund plans create a unified system for the taxation of income and consumption. In fact, Hawaii has experi-

Table 1-1
State Use of the Personal Income Tax and General Retail Sales Tax (Dollar amounts in millions)

States	Personal Income Tax Collections in 1969				General Retail Sales Tax	
	Amount	As Percentage of Federal Adjusted Gross Income in 1968	As Percentage of Federal Income Tax in 1968	Collections in 1969	Rates 1/11/71 State (Local) (Percent)	Food Exemption or Income Tax Credit
United States, Total	$7,595	2.2[1]	16.1[2]	$12,501	3.6[3]	
Alabama	75	1.2	9.8	197	4(½-2)	
Alaska	25	3.4	24.3	–	(1-5)	
Arizona	53	1.3	10.6	147	3(1-2)	
Arkansas	38	1.1	9.9	104	3	
California	1,087	1.7	13.0	1,684	4(1)	Ex.
Colorado	103	1.9	14.6	123	3(1-3)	Cr.
Connecticut	–	–	–	174	5	Ex.
Delaware	61	3.7	23.0	–	–	
Dist. of Columbia	67	3.1	19.4	58	4	[4];Cr.
Florida	–	–	–	574	4	Ex.
Georgia	139	1.4	11.2	308	3	
Hawaii	87	4.1	29.8	137	4	Cr.
Idaho	38	2.6	22.6	38	3	Cr.
Illinois	–	–	–	990	4(½-1)	
Indiana	181	1.3	9.6	349	2	Cr.

6

State					
Iowa	107	1.5	12.5	208	3	
Kansas	72	1.3	10.2	137	3	
Kentucky	108	1.7	14.0	248	5	
Louisiana	45	0.6	4.7	160	3(½-3)	
Maine	–	–	–	70	5	Ex.
Maryland	313	2.4	17.0	162	4	Ex.
Massachusetts	453	2.6	18.0	158	3	Ex.;Cr.
Michigan	390	1.5	10.3	795	4	
Minnesota	304	3.2	25.4	174	3	Ex.
Mississippi	20	0.6	5.5	174	5	
Missouri	118	1.0	7.3	296	3(½-1)	
Montana	31	2.2	18.8	–	–	
Nebraska	37	1.1	8.6	70	2½	Cr.
Nevada	–	–	–	44	2(1-1½)	
New Hampshire	3	–	–	–	–	
New Jersey	15	–	–	265	5	Ex.
New Mexico	20	1.0	8.3	83	4	
New York	2,152	3.5	23.0	699	3(1-3)	Ex.
North Carolina	240	2.3	18.9	240	3(1)	
North Dakota	14	1.2	11.5	36	4	Ex.[5]
Ohio	–	–	–	621	4(½)	
Oklahoma	48	0.9	7.1	87	2(1-2)	Ex.

Oregon	204	3.8	29.2	–	–	Ex.
Pennsylvania	–	–	–	891	6	Ex.
Rhode Island	–	–	–	72	5	
South Carolina	84	1.7	14.8	138	4	
South Dakota	–	–	–	35	4	
Tennessee	11	–	–	229	3(½-1½)	
Texas	–	–	–	441	3¼(1)	Ex.
Utah	51	2.2	19.3	65	4(½)	
Vermont	34	3.3	26.1	–	3	Ex.;Cr.
Virginia	273	2.4	18.0	185	3(1)	
Washington	–	–	–	532	4½(½)	
West Virginia	31	0.9	6.9	157	3	
Wisconsin	462	4.0	31.0	117	4	Ex.
Wyoming	–	–	–	29	3	

Sources: U.S. Bureau of the Census, *State Government Finances in 1969*; U.S. Internal Revenue Service, *Statistics of Income, Individual Income Tax Returns, 1968*; and Commerce Clearing House, *State Tax Reporter*.

Ex. = Exempt.   Cr. = Credit

[1] Local rates are shown only for those states where such tax is used fairly extensively.

[2] Weighted mean of the 35 states, and the District of Columbia imposing a broad-based personal income tax for the entire fiscal year. Maine and Illinois became personal income tax states during 1969.

[3] Median state rate (does not include local sales tax rates).

[4] Food taxed at 2% (½ the regular rate).

[5] Exemption limited to milk and milk products, and fresh and cured meats, including poultry and fish and other fresh- and salt-water animal products.

mented with a diminishing income tax credit for sales tax payments, one that declines as income rises. By exempting, in effect, the poor man's hamburger while taxing the rich man's steak it is possible to minimize the loss of state sales tax revenue while shielding low-income families from the regressive impact of this levy.

State Personal Income Tax. In the ACIR publication, *State and Local Finances—Significant Features, 1967-1970*, we spelled out in more detail the three critical tests to determine whether a state is making effective and equitable use of the personal income tax.

1. To insure fairness, the state should provide for personal exemptions at least as generous as those under the federal income tax;
2. To promote taxpayer convenience and administrative simplicity, the state should employ withholding at the source and conform the technical provisions of its law to federal provisions; and
3. To insure productivity, the state should make effective use of the income tax as evidenced by state tax collections equal either to at least 20 percent of the federal personal income tax collections in that state or to at least 2 percent of adjusted gross income as reported by state residents for federal income tax purposes.

Income tax "musts," in our judgment, do not include graduated rates because a broad-based flat rate tax can pack both a heavy revenue punch and provide a substantial degree of progression when combined with personal exemptions. Personal exemptions protect the very poor from the exactions of the tax collector and they automatically adjust tax liability for size of family. The policy on graduated tax rates is best resolved by each state legislature in light of locally prevailing circumstances. It should be noted, however, that graduated rates produce increased responsiveness of income tax collections to economic growth.

State Sales and Use Tax. In our judgment, states can make effective and fairly equitable use of a sales tax if three prime conditions are met:

1. To insure productivity, the tax base employed covers most personal services as well as retail sale of tangible items;
2. To insure fairness, some provision is made for "pulling the regressive stinger"—either an outright exemption of food and drug purchases or a system of income tax credits and cash refunds to shield subsistence income from the sales tax collector's reach; and
3. To promote taxpayer convenience and administrative simplicity, states need to credit their taxpayers for sales and use taxes paid to other states; eliminate charges for audit of multistate firms; exchange audit and other information with one another; and permit local governments to "piggyback" their levy on the state sales tax.

Smoothing Out Property Tax Assessment

To smooth out the great peaks and valleys on the property tax assessment front, the Advisory Commission in a report on *The Role of the States in Strengthening the Property Tax* offered a detailed prescription for reducing the inequities caused by faulty assessment practices. Underpinning the twenty-nine policy recommendations are the following major assumptions:

1. While a state administered assessment system should be viewed as the instrument of choice, the prevailing joint state-local system for administering the property tax can work with a reasonable degree of effectiveness if the state tax department is given sufficient executive support, legal authority, and professional stature to insure local compliance with state law calling for uniformity of tax treatment.
2. That professionalization of the assessment function can ordinarily be achieved only if the assessor is removed from the elective process and selected on the basis of demonstrated ability to appraise property.
3. That the perennial conflict between state law calling for full value assessment and the local practice of fractional assessment can be resolved most expeditiously by permitting local assessment officials to assess at any uniform percentage of current market value above a specified minimum level, provided this policy is reinforced with two important safeguards:
   a. A full disclosure policy, requiring the state tax department to make annual county assessment ratio studies and to give property owners a full report on the fractional valuation policy adopted by county assessors; and
   b. An appeal provision to specifically authorize the introduction of state assessment ratio data by the taxpayer as evidence in appeals to review agencies on the issue of whether his assessment is inequitable.

The Commission's prescription for property tax reform also calls for the repeal of the personal property tax on business inventories—a levy that probably has produced as much administrative mischief as tax revenue.

Those of us who have been beating the drums for property tax reform, however, must not forget that the single most important characteristic of a well administered property tax is the degree of assessment uniformity to be found within each taxing jurisdiction. Evidence obtained from the 1967 Census of Governments indicates that many assessors are achieving an acceptable degree of uniformity at least for residential property.

Increased reliance on the use of computers for trending assessments may soon enable us to adopt a more stringent rule of thumb for judging the uniformity of assessments. In the past, most of us accepted the coefficient of dispersion of 20 as evidence of an acceptable administrative performance. Hopefully, we will soon be in a position to scale the standard down to 15 or perhaps even to a coefficient of dispersion of 10 for residential property.

We reformers must also not overlook the fact that several states, prompted in

Table 1-2
Two Measures of Intra-Area Assessment Uniformity (Coefficient of Dispersion of Assessment Ratios for Nonfarm Houses, by State, 1966)

State	Median Measure of Dispersion[1]	Adjusted Measure of Dispersion	
		Weighted Mean[2]	Extent of Coverage[3]
United States	19.2	18.8	76%
Alabama	27.4	17.2	79
Alaska	17.3	14.6	56
Arizona	26.0	19.0	88
Arkansas	19.8	18.8	44
California	15.1	15.5	100
Colorado	19.0	14.9	86
Connecticut	12.3	12.6	28
Delaware	19.8	15.6	100
Florida	14.2	13.9	89
Georgia	16.9	15.0	71
Hawaii	25.7	17.3	93
Idaho	25.7	26.1	28
Illinois	20.3	18.5	89
Indiana	22.7	19.4	69
Iowa	18.9	14.2	49
Kansas	28.5	19.3	52
Kentucky	15.8	14.3	60
Louisiana	22.5	22.0	74
Maine	15.6	11.2	5
Maryland	16.9	14.8	86
Massachusetts	14.6	18.6	24
Michigan	20.7	15.1	30
Minnesota	22.8	22.0	83
Mississippi	27.8	24.7	50
Missouri	25.3	18.9	86
Montana	22.5	15.9	39
Nebraska	23.7	17.3	94
Nevada	19.4	12.9	91
New Hampshire	14.8	14.8	10
New Jersey	18.1	16.1	99
New Mexico	22.7	20.4	83
New York	34.3	31.5	99
North Carolina	18.2	14.8	68
North Dakota	26.8	16.4	18

Ohio	16.2	15.7	92
Oklahoma	23.2	18.1	61
Oregon	18.9	17.8	77
Pennsylvania	25.5	22.7	98
Rhode Island	14.2	13.5	36
South Carolina	33.7	31.0	75
South Dakota	22.0	20.0	36
Tennessee	19.5	17.9	73
Texas	29.0	27.0	86
Utah	21.0	18.8	87
Vermont	18.8	na	—
Virginia	15.8	10.5	65
Washington	21.7	20.5	85
West Virginia	22.9	17.8	62
Wisconsin	16.2	13.7	32
Wyoming	23.0	17.6	18

Note: The general rule of thumb holds that an intra-area coefficient of dispersion of less than 20 indicates a tolerable degree of nonuniformity.

n.a. Data not available.

[1] This measure of uniformity appears in Volume 2 of the 1967 Census of Governments, *Taxable Property Values*, Table 16.

[2] The adjusted measures of dispersion are derived by averaging the individual coefficients of dispersion on the basis of the estimated market value of nonfarm houses in each jurisdiction.

[3] Percentage of market value of all nonfarm houses accounted for by included jurisdictions.

large part by judicial action, have significantly narrowed the perennial gap between assessment law and practice. For example, Kentucky and Oregon have raised the general level of local assessments to close to the full value standard called for in those two states.

State Financed Property Tax Relief

A state's responsibility for property tax reform would not be completely discharged even if it could wave a magic wand over all local tax rolls and produce perfect assessment uniformity at the full value level. There is a second dimension to the property tax problem—the collection of this tax would still create a special hardship for property owners with low incomes.

Although the value of the family residence serves as a fairly good proxy of ability to pay taxes in a rural society, total household income stands out as a far more precise measure of taxable capacity in our modern urban society.

This point can be illustrated quickly by pointing out the hardship that the payment of residential property taxes imposes on low-income households. With retirement, the flow of income drops sharply and a $300 a year property tax bill that once could be taken in stride becomes a disproportionate claim on the income of an elderly couple living on a pension of $1,200 a year. In fact, it becomes an impossible 25 percent tax on shelter. By the same token, if the flow of income falls sharply as a result of the death or physical disability of the breadwinner, or due to unemployment, then again payment of the residential property tax can become an extraordinary tax burden.

As a result, thousands of homeowners, mostly elderly, are forced each year to liquidate part of their assets or endure real privation in order to pay the local tax on shelter. It is a bitter commentary on our youth-oriented society when the many elderly persons are forced through the property tax wringer in order to finance the education of the young.

Circuit-Breaker Approach. The most efficient method for dealing with this problem is to take the so-called "circuit-breaker" approach for protecting low-income property owners from property tax overloads. Vermont, for example, has taken the position that an elderly householder who is required to make a residential tax payment in excess of 7 percent of total family income is deemed to be carrying an excessive property tax load and the state rebates to the taxpayer that part of the payment that is in excess of the 7 percent figure.

The great virtue of the circuit-breaker approach is that it can rifle in tax relief to those who need it the most while minimizing the drawdown on state funds. Just as important, it can provide timely relief. The eligible elderly homeowner in Wisconsin does not have to pay the local property tax bill first and then wait until the next year to file a state income tax return together with a claim for rebate. In that state the elderly homeowner can file for the state tax rebate as soon as the tax bill arrives thereby permitting state aid to be extended in time to protect the homeowner or renter from excessive residential property tax burden.

In Table 1-3 I have set out the basic characteristics of the tax relief programs now administered by the five states using the circuit-breaker approach.

The efficiency of the circuit-breaker is reflected in the remarkable transformation of a regressive tax into an essentially proportional levy at relatively modest cost to the state treasury. In 1968, for example, Wisconsin aided 66,000 beneficiaries at a cost of about $6 million—this is less than 1 percent of the total property tax take and, in per capita terms, it cost less than $2 per person.

The important thing, however, is this—it extended relief to those who needed it the most, to the over 7,000 elderly householders with income less than $1,000 who had paid out in residential taxes about 30 percent on the average of their total subsistence income. In fact, the data set forth in Table 1-4 almost boggle the mind. It is difficult to conceive that in this day and age we would ever permit our tax collectors to inflict so much damage on the poor.

13

Table 1-3
State Financed and Administered Residential Property Tax Relief for Protecting Low-Income Households from Property Tax Overloads (The "Circuit-Breaker")

State	Beneficiaries Description	Income Ceiling	Tax Relief Formula	Form of Abatement and Estimated Per Capita Cost	Date of Adoption	Statutory Citation
Wisconsin	Homeowners & renters 65 & older	$3,700	See footnote[1]	State income tax credit or rebate Cost—$1.50 (1968)	1963	Chap. 71, Sec. 71.09(7)
Minnesota	Homeowners & renters age 65 & older	$3,500	Relief ranges from 75% of tax payment if household income is under $500 to 10% if family income is between $3,000 and $3,499	State income tax credit or rebate Cost—$0.50 (1968)(This aid is in addition to a general state-financed property tax relief that approximates 35% of the homeowner's tax bill)	1967	Chap. 290, Sec. 290.0601 et seq
California	Homeowners age 65 & older; no relief for renters	$3,350	Relief ranges from 95% of tax payment if household income is less than $1,000 to 1% of tax payment if household income is $3,350	State rebate only Cost—$0.40 (1969)	1967	Revenue & taxation code Div. E., Sec. 19501 et seq
Vermont	Homeowners & renters age 65 & older	Not explicit	Relief limited to that part of tax payment in excess of 7% of household income times a local rate factor that varies by tax rate of local community[2]	State income tax credit or rebate Cost—$1.25 (1969)	1969	H.B. 222
Kansas	Homeowners age 65 & older; no relief for renters	$3,700	Same as Wisconsin tax relief formula	State income tax credit or rebate	1970	H.B. 1253

[1] Household income—$1,000 or less—relief ranges from 75% of amount by which property tax exceeds 3% of household income between $500 and $1,000; household income—over $1,000—60% of amount by which property tax exceeds 3% of household income between $500 and $1,000, 6% of income between $1,000 and $1,500, 9% of income between $1,500 and $2,000, 12% of income between $2,000 and $2,500, and 15% of all household income over $2,500. The maximum property tax to be used for this credit is limited to $330.

[2] The Commissioner shall annually prepare and make available the local rate factors by arraying all municipalities according to their effective tax rate and dividing the population of the State into quintiles from such array with those having the lowest effective tax rates being in the first quintile. The local rate factors shall be as follows: first quintile, 0.6; second quintile, 0.8; third quintile, 1.0; fourth quintile, 1.2; fifth quintile, 1.4. The amount of property taxes or rent constituting property taxes used in computing the credit are limited to $300 per taxable year.

Table 1-4
The "Circuit-Breaker" System for Protecting Low-Income Households From Property Tax Overload Situations
How It Worked in Wisconsin and Minnesota in 1968

Household Income Group	Number of Claims	Average Household Income	Average Property Tax*		Percent of Tax Burden Relieved	Ratio of Property Tax* to Household Income	
			Before Credit	After Credit		Before Credit	After Credit
						%	%
Wisconsin							
$0-	102	$ 0	$333	$151	55%		
1- 499	539	381	254	98	61	66	26
500- 999	6,508	801	211	78	63	26	10
1,000-1,499	14,903	1,269	249	140	44	20	11
1,500-1,999	16,809	1,750	288	188	35	16	11
2,000-2,499	14,287	2,236	323	241	25	14	11
2,500-2,999	9,857	2,734	363	307	15	13	11
3,000-3,500	5,576	3,207	415	392	5	13	12
Minnesota						%	%
Less Than $250	192	$ 495	$164	$ 51	69%	33.4	8.8
$ 250- 499	198	434	145	38	74	19.6	6.0
500- 749	994	652	128	39	70	15.3	4.7
750- 999	2,108	891	136	42	69	12.6	6.4
1,000-1,249	2,779	1,132	143	72	50	10.9	5.5
1,250-1,499	3,666	1,380	151	76	50	9.9	5.8
1,500-1,749	3,453	1,624	160	95	41	8.9	5.3
1,750-1,999	3,828	1,880	167	100	40	8.4	5.9
2,000-2,249	3,115	2,122	179	125	30	7.7	5.3
2,250-2,499	2,879	2,375	182	127	30	7.0	5.6
2,500-2,749	2,403	2,717	190	151	21	6.7	5.4
2,750-2,999	2,189	2,875	194	155	20	6.4	5.7
3,000-3,249	1,488	3,124	200	179	10	6.4	5.7
3,250-3,499	1,270	3,368	215	193	6	6.4	5.7

Sources: Wisconsin Department of Revenue, Research Division, July 28, 1970. Minnesota Department of Taxation, *Property Tax Relief for Minnesota's Senior Citizens* (Special Report), August, 1970.
*Includes property tax portion of rent payments.

Local Income and Sales Taxes

The counsel of perfection might well direct state legislatures to deny local governments the right to impose a tax on income or sales. In order to reserve these prime revenue sources for the state, however, their legislatures must be prepared to either pick up virtually all of the local school tab or embark on a major revenue sharing adventure with local governments. One thing is clear. The local property tax can no longer serve as the primary revenue source for schools and the cities and counties.

Something has to give. In the judgment of the Commission, it should be the school financing responsibility. For this reason, the Commission has recently recommended that the states assume primary responsibility for financing public education, thereby freeing the property tax for those governmental activities that are essentially local in character: the municipal-type functions such as police and fire protection, local parks and recreation, and general government.

If a state is not willing to embark on this course of action, or to launch an unconditional revenue sharing program with its local governments, it has no alternative but to allow local policymakers the right to tap either the sales or the income tax or both. If a state decides to follow the local nonproperty tax approach it would be well advised to:

1. Limit local nonproperty taxing powers to as large taxing areas as possible, ideally coinciding with the boundaries of trading and economic areas;
2. Prescribe rules governing taxpayers, tax base, and tax rates, etc., uniformly applicable to all local taxing jurisdictions; and
3. Provide technical assistance in administering and enforcing nonproperty taxes.

Our prescription that states collect local taxes appears to be quite popular. As of January 1, 1970, local taxes were "piggybacked" on state taxes in twenty-two states:

General sales tax	18
Cigarette	2
Gasoline	3
Motor vehicle excise	1
Personal income	3
Selected excises	1
	28 taxes

Implications For the Business Community

With the exception of the specific recommendation calling for state repeal of the personal property tax on business inventories, the Commission has taken no stand on the size or the character of the state and local tax load borne by business firms.

It would be safe, however, to draw at least one clear policy inference from Commission recommendations: *Its high quality state-local tax system is designed to hurry history along by encouraging states to place relatively greater emphasis on direct personal taxes and hence relatively less weight on the indirect business-type levies.*

According to our calculations, revenue from direct personal taxes (individual income and retail sales taxes) rose from 20 percent to almost 30 percent of total state-local tax collections between 1957 and 1967. During the same period we estimate that state and local taxes with an initial impact on business fell from 34 percent to about 29 percent of total state and local tax collections, despite the fact that actual collections from the business tax sector increased during this interval by over $8 billion.[2]

Judging from this trend, business firms are becoming relatively less important as state and local taxpayers, but increasingly important as state and local tax collectors. Probably some of you are now thinking—a few more victories like this and we are ruined!

At this point, I shall sum up the case for the ACIR brand of a high quality state-local tax system by noting that each of its various components has been tested in the public finance marketplace. This is one of the truly great features of our decentralized system of government. It permits and encourages experimentation in the various fields of taxation.

From this testing process, operating in the real world of state and local financing, we can identify those tax policies that work in the right direction—that of increasing the productivity and the equity of state and local revenue systems.

Ultimately, however, our task becomes political. We must take the various components of a high quality revenue system and, to use the language of television, "put it all together."

Notes

1. *Coordination of State and Federal Inheritance, Estate and Gift Taxes* (A-1, January, 1961); *State and Local Taxation of Privately Owned Property Located in Federal Areas* (A-6, June, 1961); *Local Nonproperty Taxes and the Coordinating Role of the State* (A-9, September, 1961); *State Constitutional and Statutory Restrictions on Local Taxing Powers* (A-14, October, 1962); *The Role of the States in Strengthening the Property Tax* (A-17, June, 1963); *The Intergovernmental Aspects of Documentary Taxes* (A-23, September, 1964); *State-Federal Overlapping in Cigarette Taxes* (A-24, September, 1964); *Federal-State Coordination of Personal Income Taxes* (A-27, October, 1965); *State-Local Taxation and Industrial Location* (A-30, April, 1967); *Fiscal Balance in the*

American Federal System (A-31, October, 1967); *State Aid to Local Government* (A-34, April, 1969).

2. Advisory Commission on Intergovernmental Relations, *Estimates of State and Local Taxes Initially Paid by Business Firms, 1957-1962-1967* (September, 1970), updating estimates published in *State-Local Taxation and Industrial Location* (A-30, April, 1967).

2

An Appraisal From the Viewpoint of a State Tax Administrator

J. E. Luckett

Put in question form, the subject of this session is: "What are the characteristics of a high quality tax system?" This is a good question to ask but not so easy to answer. Our appraisal will be from the standpoint of a state tax administrator, one charged with carrying out tax law, but not one who "makes" the law. We leave it to others to develop their own specialized viewpoints—of which there are several, each important to the overall evaluation of a system.

To approach the question, let us first look at the objectives of tax policy and also the objectives of tax administration. We need some bench marks by which to establish how well or how poorly a tax or tax system, in operation, measures up to expected standards.

An old English proverb states that "the proof of the pudding is in the eating." Likewise, it may be said, the proof of a tax or tax system is in its administrative performance. Such performance includes all the communication and interaction of the administrator and the taxpayer in the tax compliance and enforcement processes.

Objectives of Tax Policy and Administration

People have been talking, and complaining, about taxes since the beginning of recorded history. In Western philosophy the idea has prevailed that taxation should be equitable and just. Adam Smith is remembered for his "Canons of Taxation" included in *The Wealth of Nations*, published in 1776. Smith's canons or objectives, reinterpreted and couched in a modern version, might be stated as follows:

A tax policy program should:
1. Provide adequate revenue.
2. Distribute the burden equitably.
3. Be understandable and convenient for taxpayers.
4. Permit efficient, economical administration.
5. Promote good social and economic effects.

19

The objectives of tax administration are essentially the same as those of tax policy but with a different focus, and with major emphasis on points three and four. The role of the administrator is different from that of the policymaker, although there are situations when, through the rule-making process, the administrator may be said to "make policy," as a function of administrative authority and discretion.

What we have in mind is the role of the administrator, not as putting flesh and blood on the bones of the basic tax law—it is partly that as any state tax administrator knows—but in serving as a middleman, the communicating link between the policymakers (such as governor and legislature, or mayor and council) and the taxpayers. In this role he is a kind of educational broker; an expert advisor; a patient instructor; an architect and engineer of forms and procedures; an enforcement officer when the need arises; a public relations spokesman on how, and how well, a given policy may, or should, work out in practice.

In such a role, a state tax administrator has three obligations:

1. Execute existing law as firmly, efficiently, and equitably as possible.
2. Report to the governor, legislature, and public on his stewardship.
3. Identify, in detail, specific problems which may defeat the long run objectives or intent of a given tax policy.

If tax law cannot be efficiently, effectively, and equitably enforced it is bad law and should be changed. The law, however, is not always the villain. Administration may be the weak link in the chain. The tax conference literature is filled with criticism by businessmen, tax scholars, and others of many aspects of such basic taxes as those on income, sales, and property; and, there is much to criticize, both as to policy and administration.

The analyzed experience of business taxpayers and tax administrators has much to tell about what constitutes "good" and "bad" law, and also what constitutes good and bad administration. What does experience tell us about quality, or the lack of it?

Specific Characteristics
of a Quality System

One can think of many characteristics of a good system, both as to policy and administration. Among such, and strictly from the administrator's standpoint, we would consider the following five characteristics to be of major importance, whether the orientation is to business, or to the individual citizen:

1. Revenue as the prime goal—not social or economic objectives.
2. Clearly written tax law and regulations.

3. Uniform standards and definitions.
4. Effective enforcement.
5. Healthy administrative environment.

Let us examine each characteristic in some detail.

Revenue as the Prime Goal

If revenue is to be the primary goal, tax policy should be unencumbered as much as possible. Exceptions create administrative problems.

The paramount obligation of the tax administrator is to execute the tax laws as efficiently and equitably as possible. He can fulfill this obligation much more effectively if those responsible for formulating basic tax policy do not lose sight of the primary function of a tax system—that of revenue production. When tax policy becomes burdened with too much emphasis on social or economic objectives (granted their importance) the ability to provide efficient and equitable administration can be seriously impaired.

When the objective of tax policy is to promote some social or economic purpose, the tax is not only difficult to administer with fairness, but very often the intended worthy purpose becomes discriminatory in application.

Consider the current emphasis on tax subsidies for pollution control facilities. One hears much discussion about the desirability of tax incentives to encourage business to install such facilities. However, many businesses have already installed very expensive pollution control equipment without the benefit of a tax subsidy. Unless legislation has retroactive provisions to give the same benefit to those who have voluntarily demonstrated good corporate citizenship, discrimination results, not to mention lost revenue and the difficulty of precise determination of exemptions or credits affecting the given facilities.

When features of this type are written into the tax laws, the tax administrator is often faced with the responsibility of interpreting ambiguous terms and his decisions often must be based on technical consideration as to the use or function of certain property. Under these circumstances, tax decisions may be influenced by the expertise of articulate company technicians in explaining operational functions.

Do businesses need a tax subsidy to stop polluting the air and water? If so, in light of the problems inherent in providing "tax incentives," it may be preferable to provide direct open government subsidies instead, measured by appropriate industry differentials in production volume, or resources used, or some other yardstick.

Clearly Written Tax Law

In a high quality tax system, perhaps the most basic ingredient is the tax law itself. It should be conceived and constructed in a manner which makes the intent as clear as possible. It is most important in the formulation of state and local tax law that ample hearings and discussions be held in order to have the benefit of different viewpoints. Moreover, full disclosure of intent of sponsors is not always too apparent to lawmakers, or administrators, let alone the public. The minutes of such hearings are often valuable to tax administrators.

Tax law should be devoid of ambiguous terminology. Ambiguity leads to controversy; and controversy leads to litigation—expensive for both government and the taxpayer.

The law should be complete and precise as to all substantive matters, but flexible enough to allow sufficient administrative discretion in application, particularly through the rule-making process.

For example, tax laws generally provide penalties for various taxpayer violations. Should penalties be mandatory, or should tax administrators have discretionary powers in applying penalties? Penalties for certain violations perhaps should be mandatory. But in many cases the tax administrator will be able to administer the tax more efficiently and equitably if given discretionary powers, subject to rigid supervision, in the application of penalties.

Uniform Standards and Definitions

We hear the word "uniformity" mentioned often in tax circles. It is particularly significant to the businessman and for good reason. Uniform definitions, among federal, state, and local jurisdictions, especially in regard to income taxes, are extremely helpful to the taxpayer.

Often, multistate businesses must be concerned with the tax laws of many states and many local taxing jurisdictions.

Uniformity among the states (and local governments) in jurisdictional rules for income and sales taxes and in the apportionment of income for income tax purposes is vitally important. The significance of this subject is illustrated by the current interest shown by the United States Congress and pending proposals for federal legislation affecting the taxation of interstate business.

States have made notable progress. For instance, some twenty-two states have now adopted the Uniform Division of Income for Tax Purposes Act (UDITPA). Much more needs to be done.

Effective Enforcement

Although the structure of the tax law and the tax policy with regard to uniform standards are vitally important, the actual "success" or "failure" of a tax system may well depend upon the effectiveness of enforcement practices. Nothing will do more to destroy public confidence, encourage taxpayer apathy, and invite outright tax evasion than a poorly conceived, haphazard, enforcement policy.

Audit Program. A well planned and well executed audit program utilizing competent auditors and sound techniques is essential to effective enforcement. Periodic audit of all taxpayers is desirable.

What is the purpose of auditing a taxpayer's records? Is the purpose to uncover tax deficiencies? Yes, but not entirely. In a high quality tax system, the overriding issue in the performance of an audit should be that of determining correct tax liability under the law, without prejudice as to whether the audit results in a tax deficiency or overpayment of tax.

Under no circumstance should the amount of additional revenue produced by an auditor be an important factor in the evaluation of the auditor's overall performance.

Audits should be scheduled well in advance; and taxpayer convenience should be served whenever possible.

A taxpayer should not be expected to open his books and records to inspection for income tax purposes one week and then a little later receive notice that he is to be audited by the same jurisdiction for sales and use taxes. If each auditor is not trained to audit for the different taxes imposed by a taxing jurisdiction, then the joint or team audit approach should be used, under which the income tax auditor and the sales tax auditor collaborate.

Intergovernmental Exchange of Information. Enforcement procedures are improved through a system of exchange of information—between federal and state, between different states, and between state and local governments. This sometimes makes it possible to eliminate some of the detail of taxpayer reporting and decreases duplication of effort.

State Supervision of the Property Tax. Because of the revenue importance of the property tax to business and to local governments, as well as to some state governments, special comment is warranted. Probably no single tax suffers more from inadequate and inequitable administration, particularly at the local level, than the property tax.

Earlier we discussed the importance of uniform standards. However, in the property tax field standards are not lacking. State statutes are filled with standards that either are generally ignored or administered more or less capriciously. The exceptions are so few, judging from United States Census and related studies, that one wonders how such an important tax can suffer such a divergence between law and practice.

The alleged inherent deficiencies and administrative infeasibilities of this tax are often emphasized. Some scholars think the classified form of the property tax makes for a potentially better result. However, there are numerous deficiencies insofar as this policy relates to the business sector.

Taxing real estate only may perhaps be a better approach; however, statistical evidence generated by the Census Bureau, state governments, and various university research agencies have shown serious inter- and intra-area and class inequities. The limitations posed by such inequities severely limit the usefulness of the tax as a prime revenue source when relative fairness among taxpayers is a paramount consideration.

Progress on the assessment front is slow and spotty. Marked improvement has been made most often in those areas where administration is based upon good law providing for effective supervision and where the assessment authorities maintain good facilities, exercise a high degree of leadership, and receive strong support from the business community and from taxpayers generally.

Those taxpayers, business or otherwise, who meet their legal responsibilities have an absolute right to expect that all others be required to fulfill their legal responsibilities.

The Advisory Commission on Intergovernmental Relations has done much to stimulate improvement among the states by recommending legislation embodying the best features of property tax law dealing with organization and administration. And the International Association of Assessing Officers and the National Association of Tax Administrators have done much to encourage professionalism among assessors.

If there is to be greater statewide equity in the property tax, whatever the given tax base, the following essentials must be provided: effective state supervision over the local assessment process; trained assessors (preferably appointed); and appropriate tools for property identification and valuation—tax maps and other record systems necessary to provide adequate documentation for assessments. But a professional approach and an unwillingness to be swayed by those concerned with private rather than public interests lies at the heart of the problem.

Healthy Administrative Environment

We have considered the objectives of a tax system, the need for a clearly written tax law, the desirability of uniform standards among taxing jurisdictions, and the importance of an effective enforcement program. But, in considering the overall characteristics of a high quality state and local tax system, the tax administrator must look one step further. Again his primary obligation is to execute the law as efficiently and equitably as possible. If he is to succeed, he needs to be able to operate within a healthy administrative environment. What constitutes such an environment? Let us consider four essential elements:

1. Efficient organization and management.
2. Qualified personnel.
3. Good technical facilities.
4. Professional motivation.

Efficient Organization and Management. Governments can take their cue from business in terms of organization. Those businesses which succeed are also those which are noted for their organizational system and continuing top quality management. Organization at the state level will be more efficient if the administrative structure is integrated and functional rather than compartmentalized, tax by tax for the common functions.

Lines of authority and functional responsibilities must be clearly defined. The system of supervision should be well understood. Every employee in the organization should know who his boss is and should report only to that boss.

The chief tax administrator must have ample time to deal with management problems and not get bogged down in matters that should be handled by subordinates. This requires attention to the proper delegation of duties and assignment of responsibilities.

The system of internal communications and reporting must be adequate in order for management to know what is going on and to maintain effective supervision. Manpower and equipment should be utilized so as to assure maximum production and a minimum of idle time.

The possibility of irregularities and errors must be minimized through an effective system of internal audit and control.

Qualified Personnel. Job specifications and testing procedures must be adequate to assure that each new employee meets minimum standards. Effective training programs, in-service workshops, and college sponsored seminars encourage employee development. A system of periodic evaluation and rating of employees' performance is important. Employee morale and efficiency are enhanced through a system of promotion based on performance and salaries competitive with those offered by other employers. Few states measure up. It is to the best interest of business and taxpayers generally to have quality personnel in government tax jobs.

Good Technical Facilities. The tax administrator should have adequate equipment and facilities. This does not necessarily mean that the latest or most expensive data processing machines are required. Adequate space is a necessity and is important to employee morale and efficiency. Good organization, based on work flow and time and motion studies, can help alleviate the problem of limited space.

Professional Motivation. A healthy administrative environment requires good organization and management, good personnel, and adequate technical facilities. Yet the presence of these factors alone will not assure the type of environment that is so urgently needed. A further requirement, and certainly not the least in importance, may be termed "professional motivation." To me it means the presence of a professional atmosphere throughout that is continuously demonstrated by the performance of the organization. It requires that each and every decision, whether it is hiring and promotion of personnel, answering the complaint of an individual taxpayer, or auditing the largest corporation, is based squarely on professional considerations.

The term also signifies an attitude—a special kind of pride which must prevail throughout the organization, from the chief tax administrator to the lowest paid clerk. The rewards are many for the tax administrator who will not compromise this point.

A professionally motivated well organized system of administration will produce optimum results for any given tax system.

Summary

The heart of what has been said above may be summarized as follows: The characteristics of a high quality tax system include the ability to collect all taxes which any person or business may be required by law to pay, but no more; to recognize tax administration as a professional and technical task calling for competent personnel; to develop an efficiently functioning organization; to cultivate helpful relationships with other governmental agencies; and to merit the respect and confidence of the taxpayers. These are the principles by which the tax agency should be guided in performing its public services.

3 An Appraisal From One Business Viewpoint

F. J. Siska, Jr.

In expressing one business viewpoint of a high quality state and local tax system, I have attempted to be objective. The thoughts herein are my own and may or may not be those of my employer or of any particular segment of the business community.

Certainly the business community recognizes the fundamental need for state and local governmental units to raise revenue to support the necessary services and functions they are called upon to perform. As a corollary, it has genuine interest, as do all taxpayers, in assuring that revenues generated are commensurate with the realistic cost of necessary governmental programs. Equally certain is the general willingness of the business community as taxpayers to bear a fair share of the burden. Unfortunately, the divergence of definitions of "fair share" sometimes approaches infinity, particularly so among multistate taxpayers.

There is considerably more community of position among businessmen relative to problems related to fulfilling the function of tax collector. Coming from a retailing background, my approach to general sales and use taxes is first as a tax collector and secondarily as a taxpayer.

General Sales and Use Tax

In the sales tax area we agree with the Advisory Commission on Intergovernmental Relations position that the tax base should be as broad as possible, including the taxation of personal services. A broad-based sales tax can be a tremendous revenue producer and is less likely to be discriminatory.

From a practical standpoint, however, drafting a broad-based sales tax acceptable to everyone can be quite difficult. A broad-based bill taxing almost all services was introduced in the Illinois General Assembly a few years ago. The resulting stampede of protesters to Springfield convinced the General Assembly that the bill needed some amendments. The bill was amended to tax only four service occupations instead of virtually all of them. The Illinois Supreme Court struck down the law on the basis that selecting a few services to tax was unreasonable.

I agree with the drafting approach used by the ACIR in their suggested retail sales tax. The services taxed are specifically enumerated, and while the base is broad, it does not include services that would tend to make the proposed bill controversial.

The regressiveness of the sales tax has been discussed and argued about for years. I shall not comment on the question of just how regressive a sales tax is. However, assuming the sales tax is regressive and unfair, business generally prefers a system of income tax credits or cash refunds to eliminate any unfair burdens. Generally speaking, the retailer prefers the fewest possible outright exemptions under a sales tax. A selective sales tax places a practical burden on the retailer. One example that comes to mind occurred in one state, under its former selective sales tax. Work clothing was exempt and recreational clothing was taxable. We constantly had the problem of a customer buying hunting clothing such as a hat, pants, or boots to be worn in "construction" work.

Compliance Problems

The point I would like to make is that the compliance problems encountered by a retailer should also be given consideration along with the desire to eliminate unfair aspects of a sales tax.

Since federal legislation regarding the taxation of interstate commerce has been proposed, the states have virtually eliminated two practices that were objectionable to business. One was the failure to allow a credit for sales and use taxes paid to another state and the second was elimination of the charges for auditing a multistate firm.

The taxability of freight charges is another problem area that current proposed federal legislation has addressed itself to and that is currently being discussed among many of the states through the Multistate Tax Commission and other channels. Under the existing state laws, tax on freight charges can be excluded under a variety of circumstances. The taxability of freight charges can be dependent on (1) when title passes to the buyer; (2) whether freight is separately billed; (3) whether the charges have been separately contracted for; (4) whether the carrier is the seller or some other person; and (5) whether the charges are billed to the buyer by the seller or by the carrier.

Some states apply only one of these standards, others apply a combination of factors to determine taxability. One state, Louisiana, includes all freight charges when imposing the use tax, but allows an exclusion under the sales tax for freight charges incurred after title passes. The existence of different procedures for each state greatly increases the complexities of proper tax compliance. Furthermore, the different standards can and do produce discriminatory results. We are hopeful that the problems associated with freight charges will be eliminated through federal legislation or through voluntary state action.

Expansion of Local Sales Taxes

One of the growing problem areas for business in the sales and use field is rapid expansion of local taxes. Some of the problems associated with local sales and use tax compliance are: (1) multiplicity of returns; (2) lack of proper information; and (3) determination of the tax base, rates, and collection procedures. These problems are more typically associated with the locally administered sales tax. Another large problem also existing in the state-administered sales taxes is assigning the sale to the proper jurisdiction and the corresponding record-keeping on the part of the seller. A postal address is no assurance of the locality entitled to the tax. There is also the problem of city boundaries being changed through annexation.

From a business standpoint, the state-administered "piggyback" system of local taxation is preferred without question. Under a state-administered system the only major problem is the allocation of sales by locality, and this certainly can be a problem under certain systems.

Probably business would prefer to have the state distribute a portion of the sales tax to localities on a statistical or formula basis such as population or a combination of factors. This system has been adopted in several states, thereby relieving the seller of the burden of localizing the sale or the destination of the sale.

Another approach that has proved to be less burdensome than most is the Illinois system. Illinois localities have not been given the power to adopt a use tax. Local collections are assigned on the basis of where the order is accepted. This, in effect, requires an allocation only to those localities where the seller has a business location. It also eliminates the necessity of the record-keeping associated with out-of-city deliveries to substantiate nontaxable sales where the sale is assigned to a locality on a destination basis. The local tax system wherein the seller encounters both a sales and use tax certainly is the most difficult for the multistate seller to comply with.

With the growing pressure for revenue at the local level and the tendency of state government to shift the political burden of increasing taxes, local taxes can only increase in the future. Illinois voters will consider a new constitution on December 15 of this year. This constitution, if adopted,[a] will grant home rule units the power to tax with certain limitations. The local sales tax system, along with its ease of compliance, could undergo substantial change. I think business generally agrees with the conclusion of the 1969 report of the Illinois Governor's Revenue Study Committee, concerning home rule powers. Their conclusion was that localities should not be permitted to impose separate taxes and "the state should impose uniform income, sales and commodity taxes but with adequate

[a]Adopted by voters; effective July 1, 1971.

provisions for sharing revenues. The way to meet the increasing fiscal problems of local governments is by sharing revenues rather than by allowing local governments to create chaotic disturbances in administration, in tax reporting, and in trade by rendering otherwise good taxes non-uniform in their impact."[1]

Jurisdictional Standards
and Collection Requirements

Another area in the sales and use tax system that has been in the spotlight recently is the multistate vendor and the compliance problems associated with jurisdictional standards and collection requirements.

There is no single source or guideline that may be used to determine under what circumstances a seller is required to collect a use tax. Also, unlike the income tax, there is no federal statutory law in the area of interstate use tax collection. To determine a prescribed jurisdictional standard, and whether it is a valid one, it is generally necessary to examine the state statutes, the regulations under the statutes, the Federal Constitution, and the court cases interpreting the Constitution.

However, since the United States Supreme Court's decision in *National Bellas Hess*,[2] it would appear that in order to justify seller collection requirements, there must be a physical use of state facilities. This decision has limited the state's jurisdiction and, of course, eliminated a segment of revenue available to the state.

The Rodino bill, H.R. 7906, would impose a further limit to the jurisdictional powers of the states. Under this bill, a state could not require a seller to collect a sales or use tax unless the seller has a business location in the state or regularly makes household deliveries in the state. This bill, if enacted, would legislatively overrule the *General Trading*[3] decision and the *Scripto*[4] decision. You will recall that in *General Trading*, the court held that their presence in Iowa through traveling employee salesmen was sufficient contact to confer jurisdiction. In *Scripto* the rule in the *General Trading* case was extended to require use tax collection where the seller made sales through independent brokers in the state.

I submit that, just as a requirement for a quality sales tax demands a broad base, the jurisdictional base must also be as broad as the practical capability of enforcement and the burden of compliance will permit, limited further, of course, by due process considerations. I further submit, that the Rodino bill in seeking the goal of uniformity and certainty will unnecessarily restrict the state's power to tax and further will create a competitive disadvantage. The loss in revenue and discrimination between vendors seem to be greater than the burden placed on interstate commerce.

The Murphy-Cranston bill, S. 3368, on the other hand, would codify the *General Trading* and *Scripto* cases. This would preserve existing revenue for the states and in an area proven to be capable of enforcement. The Rodino bill applies the business location and household delivery standard to the requirements for classifying sales for local purposes. I believe that the local jurisdictional standard should be identical to the state jurisdictional standard. Since the Murphy-Cranston bill is preferable at the state level, these same standards should be made applicable to local taxes.

The Rodino bill would, however, for all practical purposes, eliminate unjust discrimination among border retailers. The retailer with locations on both sides of the border is required to collect the tax, and if he cannot collect the tax because competition will not permit it, he must absorb the tax. The household delivery provision will require the retailer not having a place of business, but making household deliveries, to collect the tax as imposed by the destination state.

Concepts of a Quality Sales Tax

To sum up, a quality sales and use tax system should incorporate the following concepts and ideas:

1. The tax should be broad based.
2. It should contain as few exemptions as possible.
3. Provisions to lessen the regressiveness should be in the form of an income tax credit or cash refund.
4. The trend to eliminate complex or discriminatory aspects of the state's statutes should continue, particularly in the area of freight charges.
5. Local taxes at the very minimum should be state administered and based on the state sales tax law. Preferably, the state should share and distribute revenue to local jurisdictions on a formula or statistical basis.
6. In the interstate area, the jurisdictional base should be as broad as both the capability of enforcement and the burden of compliance will permit.
7. Discrimination in the border market areas should be eliminated by the adoption of the household delivery standard at the federal level.

Local Property Tax

Now I would like to say a few words about property tax administration, particularly the Advisory Commission report on *The Role of the State in Strengthening the Property Tax*. This report makes many excellent recommendations that I am sure have found widespread support.

Business certainly endorses the overall policy of the Advisory Commission and shares the goal of reducing inequities caused by poor assessing practices. The revenue yield alone in the prevailing joint state-local system for administration of the property tax assures the interest of the business community.

The property tax contrasts with income and sales taxes, which are related to market transactions, in that it depends to a large extent on human judgment.

There is a direct relationship between the quality of local administration and the degree of training and experience available to that administration. Unless local assessors have the degree of training required to assess property, all other attempts to improve the property tax system must fall short of their goal. The professionalization of the local assessment function cannot be overemphasized as quality judgments are the foundation of the system.

The second area that I would like to mention briefly is classification interwoven with the fractional assessment of property which businesss generally opposes. Ratios used should be determined by a state study and these ratios should be published. The taxpayer should then have the right to use these ratios as a basis to protest the equity of his assessment.

Corporate Income Tax

The second major area of business involvement as a taxpayer is the corporate income tax, and this is the area concerning which there is the greatest divergence of opinion. As the problems in the income tax area are too numerous to cover in the time allowed, I shall limit my comments to a few of the principal points: jurisdiction, taxable income, and apportionment.

Jurisdiction

Perhaps as a result of the fact that the company which employs me is active in all fifty states and the District of Columbia, my position on jurisdiction may be closely related to that of the tax administrators.

To the extent that any corporation "taps" the market within any taxing jurisdiction, it is in competition with all other corporations conducting a similar business therein. To the extent that it does not pay a proportionate share of the community's corporation income tax, it has a competitive advantage. I am, therefore, in favor of minimal jurisdictional restrictions and could support the standards set forth in the latest proposal of the Multistate Tax Commission.

As you are aware, P.L. 86-272 has set the income tax jurisdictional standards for the last eleven years. In essence it prohibits the imposition of an income tax on an out-of-state corporation if the corporation's only business connection with the state is the solicitation of orders by employees or independent contractors.

The Willis bill did not repeal P.L. 86-272 but set more specific jurisdictional standards for corporations having an average annual income of $1 million or less. It required a "business location" in the state and provided that:

A person shall be considered to have a business location within a State only if that person—
(1) owns or leases real property within the State,
(2) has one or more employees located in the State, or
(3) regularly maintains a stock of tangible personal property in the State for sales in the ordinary course of its business.

The Rodino bill, which passed the United States House of Representatives in 1969, extended the jurisdictional requirements of the Willis bill to all corporations regardless of size.

The latest proposal of the Multistate Tax Commission incorporates the provisions of P.L. 86-272 by reference. However, it further provides that notwithstanding the limitation of P.L. 86-272 if a corporation or any affiliated group has sales in any taxable year of more than $300,000 in a particular state, and such corporation or affiliated group has had total sales in excess of $2 million in that year and in each of the three prior years, it shall be subject to the jurisdiction of that state for that year.

While the standards set by P.L. 86-272 are not completely definitive, they now have had nationwide application for eleven years. The proposed addition of the quantitative standard in the Multistate Tax Commission plan will, if anything, minimize possible litigation concerning the application of P.L. 86-272 and minimize inequitable competition.

Taxable Income

Once jurisdiction over the taxpayer has been established, the next step is to establish the tax base. P.L. 86-272, the Willis bill, and the Rodino bill leave the determination of taxable income to the individual state. The objections to each state imposing an income tax on a different tax base are obvious.

The latest Multistate Tax Commission proposal uses as a base taxable income as determined for federal income tax purposes with certain additions and deletions. The advantages of using federal taxable income as a starting point by all states are equally obvious.

The latest proposal[b] of the Multistate Tax Commission presents workable solutions to many of the problems involved in the determination of the tax base. I shall comment briefly on the proposed solutions of some of the most controversial of these problems.

Dividends received in cash or in property from the earnings and profits of a corporation owned 80 percent or more by a recipient corporation would be eliminated from the tax base. This represents a compromise between the position of the state administrators who wish to include all dividends in the tax base and those state administrators and business corporations who wish to eliminate

[b]Based on discussions held at a Denver, Colorado, meeting in October, 1970.

all dividends from the tax base. I recognize there may be no justification for treating dividends received from 80 percent owned corporations differently than dividends received from other corporations. I feel all dividends should be eliminated from the tax base. However, I recognize that compromise is necessary.

Combination or consolidation would be at the election of either the taxing state or the taxpayer, but would be limited to affiliates. Two or more corporations are affiliated if:

1. They are component members of the same affiliated group as defined in Section 1563 of the Internal Revenue Code (80 percent ownership), and
2. They are not one of the types of corporations specifically excluded; such as financial organizations, public utilities, insurance companies, investment companies, etc., or
3. They are not corporations, substantially all of the income of which is derived from sources outside of the United States. Substantially all of the corporation's income is deemed to be derived from sources outside the United States if, upon the basis of the apportionment formula, less than 10 percent of its income for the current and each of the two preceding years is attributable to its United States activities.

I am aware that many business corporations and even some state administrators are opposed to combined reporting, while on the other hand some state administrators are almost adamant in their requirement that controlled corporations be combined. However, the Multistate Tax Commission proposal appears to be a reasonable and hopefully acceptable compromise.

Allocation and Apportionment

The Multistate Tax Commission's proposal does away with the concepts of business and nonbusiness income. All income not excluded from taxation is to be apportioned on the basis of a three-factor formula. While this would result in some shifting of the tax base between the states, it is a reasonable resolution of the problems that have arisen from the disagreements between taxpayers and state administrators as to what constitutes nonbusiness income.

The apportionment formula contained in the Multistate Tax Commission's proposal has several questionable areas. Property located in a state that has no jurisdiction to impose an income tax on the corporation would be eliminated from the denominator of the factor. The receipts factor is based on receipts from activities in the ordinary course of the taxpayer's business. It provides for a throwback of sales if the ultimate destination is in a state that has no jurisdiction to tax the corporation. The formula also provides not only for the elimination of a factor with a zero denominator, but also for the elimination of any factor with a negligible denominator. Rules are provided for determining when the denominator is negligible.

While there may be lack of agreement in principle with the elimination of any property from the denominator of the apportionment formula, with the throwback rule and with the elimination of any factor other than one with a zero denominator, it is my belief that the quantitative standard for jurisdiction set forth in the Multistate Tax Commission proposal minimizes these problems. Hopefully, they can readily be accepted by the business community.

A solution to the problem of taxation of interstate income is not a simple task. There is as much or more disagreement among state tax administrators and among the various segments of the business community as there is between the tax administrators and the business community.

The Multistate Tax Commission proposals still require some refinement. However, these proposals represent giant strides in bringing together the tax administrators and the business community. We should support the aims and direction currently taken by the Multistate Tax Commission in these proposals and trust that they will form the basis for enactment of a uniform law.

All of my comments have been directed to income taxes imposed at the state level. I have made no comments on an income tax imposed at a municipal level. This is a subject in itself and too complex to discuss in the time allowed.

Notes

1. Illinois Governor's Revenue Study Committee, *Report 1968-69*, Springfield, 1969, p. 60.

2. National Bellas Hess, Inc. v. Department of Revenue, 386 U.S. 753 (1967).

3. General Trading Co. v. State Tax Commission, 322 U.S. 335 (1944).

4. Scripto, Inc. v. Carson, 362 U.S. 207 (1960).

State and Local Taxation of Business: An Economist's Viewpoint

Frederick D. Stocker

I have been asked to give an economist's viewpoint on our topic, "The Characteristics of a High Quality State–Local Tax Structure and Its Business Tax Components." It is of course well known that economists' views on almost any subject vary widely. In particular, economists differ among themselves as to how broadly their subject should be conceived. Some public finance economists take what might be called the broad view of their subject, concerning themselves not only with the economic effects of state and local business taxes but also their administrative aspects, the problem of taxpayer compliance, legal and constitutional issues, and even the political aspects. In contrast, the narrow view of the scope of the economist's concern confines attention to those aspects that are peculiarly economic—especially the effects on resource allocation and efficiency.

My natural inclination is toward the broad view. In my opinion no public finance economist can hope to be relevant to the process of tax policy making if his scope of concern does not extend to such practical—though perhaps strictly speaking, noneconomic—considerations as those I have mentioned. However, for me to do what comes naturally would lead me onto ground that has already been ably covered by my fellow panelists. Accordingly I shall resist that temptation and center my remarks on the economic effects of state and local business taxes, and particularly on their efficiency of resource allocation.

Efficiency is the central concern of economics—efficiency in the sense of using limited resources in such a way as to get the most out of them. A well established body of economic analysis, its lineage tracing back to Adam Smith, suggests that by and large the market system, operating through private producers and consumers, all seeking to advance their own interests, will tend to produce that pattern of production and consumption that best conforms to what the members of that society want.

Neutrality as a Principle of Business Taxation

A corollary of this analysis is that whenever any policy or action interferes with or distorts the working of the market system, there is a presumption that this policy or action moves us farther away from the optimal use of resources, rather

37

than closer to it. As applied to taxation, there is, in other words, a presumption in favor of neutrality. The more nearly neutral a tax is in its effect on private decisions—methods of production, choice of a business location, factor combinations, form of business organization, marketing and distribution methods, and patterns of final consumption—the less it will interfere with attaining the theoretical optimum.

Now, we know of course that there are innumerable sources of imperfection in the working of the market system. The prevalence of elements of monopoly, lack of full knowledge on the part of buyers and sellers, immobility of resources, many kinds of legal intervention in the market place (not to mention *illegal* intervention), and sheer inertia on the part of buyers and sellers, offer good reason to question how well the market system serves the general interest. Perhaps in light of all the other distortions we need not worry very much about the additional interference with economic signals that state and local taxation cause. Yet the fact is that the market system, based on private ownership of property, free enterprise, and competition, remains the dominant force shaping our pattern of production, income distribution, and consumption. And our ideological commitment to the market system is stronger still, amounting almost to a religion. Whatever thwarts or interferes with the normal market outcome is therefore at least suspect, if not downright sinful.

Role of Nonneutral Taxes

While there may be good reasons, practical as well as ideological, for allowing the market to work freely, recognition of the highly imperfect nature of our market system tells us that a policy that might be optimal in a perfectly functioning economy may be the wrong policy, an inefficient one, if certain necessary conditions in other parts of the economy are not present. The optimal policy in an imperfect economy, in other words, may be something different from what it would be in a freely functioning competitive market system. In connection with tax policy, the point is that nonneutral taxation may occasionally be appropriate to correct for the effects of distortions within the market system. The current attention being given to the possible uses of taxation to discourage activities that cause pollution of the environment illustrates this use of nonneutral taxation in such a way as to offset other market imperfections, in this case the failure of the market to internalize all the costs of production.

In a slightly different category, nonneutral taxes sometimes play a role in advancing some social policy—the investment credit to encourage more rapid growth, tobacco and alcoholic beverage taxes to penalize disapproved forms of corruption. I do not wish here to debate the use of taxation deliberately *because* of its effects on resource allocation. For purposes of my present discussion let me define nonneutrality to include only *unintended* side effects that taxes have on the allocation and use of economic resources.

Criteria for Business Taxes

To summarize this portion of the argument, economic theory points to the following two criteria for evaluating state and local business taxes from the narrowly economic standpoint of their effect on economic efficiency:

1. In general it may be presumed that the well-being of society is best served by neutrality in taxation.
2. Where nonneutral forms of taxation are chosen, there should be convincing cause to believe that the effects on balance will advance the well-being of society rather than impair it. Haphazard, capricious, or unintended interferences with market processes, in other words, are best avoided.

Without going into the intricacies of economic theory, I would further suggest that these criteria suggest several specific guidelines in regard to business tax policy.

1. Business taxes should add to cost of production an amount as close as possible to the value of the governmental resources used in the productive process. Free public services, or charges that are less than cost, amount to a subsidy; taxes not matched by public services deter production. In either case the result is distortion.
2. Among taxes not related to costs of public services, those that fall on an "economic surplus" are most nearly neutral. Taxes that fall entirely on monopoly profits would fit this description. So would a tax on economic rent or on the site value of land.
3. Of other taxes, those not related to cost of public services or imposed on economic surplus, the most neutral are those that apply alike to the contribution all factors of production make to total output or income. The value-added tax comes to mind.

Some of the Major Areas of Nonneutrality in State-Local Business Taxation

Having sketched out what tax neutrality means, why neutral taxes are presumed to be preferable from an economic standpoint, and the general characteristic of neutral taxes, let me turn to an examination of the major business taxes used by state and local governments, noting what seem to me to be the principal departures from neutrality in each.

The Property Tax

The property tax is by far the most important state-local business tax, in terms of dollar liabilities. According to the Advisory Commission on Intergovernmental Relations, property taxes accounted for well over half, $10.3 billion, of the $17.9 billion in taxes with an initial impact on business.[1] It was the largest single business tax in every state except Delaware and West Virginia. There were thirty-four states (besides the District of Columbia) in which property taxes represented more than half of the state-local taxes impacting on business.

Now, economic theory suggests that, insofar as what in economics are called "short run" decisions are concerned, the property tax is highly neutral. With the exception of inventories, the business property tax base consists predominantly of assets that do not change either in quantity or value as a result of day-to-day or week-to-week actions. As a result, property tax costs are unaffected by most short run business decisions, and so cannot affect the outcome of the decision-making process. They do, of course, like other fixed costs, affect the overall profit or loss picture, but they do not affect the relative profitability of alternative short run courses of action.

In the long run—defined in economics as a period of time long enough to permit adjustments in fixed factors such as equipment and plant, or relocations of plant—the property tax has egregious discriminatory and market-distorting effects. As an annual charge on fixed factors, land and capital, it raises their cost relative to nontaxed inputs, thereby altering the relative profitability of alternative methods of production. As applied to land, an ad valorem tax properly administered would be expected to cause a decline in value equal to the capitalized value of the stream of tax payments. The total cost of using the land would not change, the added tax cost being offset by a reduction in rent to the owner. But as the property tax applies to physical capital—structures, equipment, and inventories—the tendency would be to discourage capital-intensive methods relative to labor-intensive methods. The property tax, in the same way, adds to the cost of improving, rehabilitating, and modernizing structures, including industrial and commercial as well as residential.

With respect to the relative cost of alternative factor combinations, it is worth noting that the increased cost of capital inputs caused by the property tax is in some degree matched by what federal payroll taxes add to the cost of labor inputs. The resulting net effect on altering factor combinations may be rather small in many instances.

Another discriminatory feature of the property tax is found in those states that tax some but not all of the capital used in business. As long as the property tax applies not only to land but to what the economist calls capital, the principle of neutrality suggests that all categories of capital should be taxed alike. Exemption of inventories, for example, whatever merit it may have on administrative grounds, results in a nonneutrality between this form of capital and others.

Any catalog of the ways in which the property tax offends against the principle of neutrality must certainly mention inequalities in assessment. These may be unintentional or they may be deliberate. It is no secret that some businesses are able to negotiate very favorable assessments—the effect of which is to give

them an advantage over less fortunate competitors in the same or other jurisdictions, and this favoritism in turn tends to distort the pattern of resource use.
Other businesses, especially those with low mobility and little political muscle,
are often deliberately assessed at discriminatory high levels, with the same distorting effect.

Finally, mention must be made of the market distortion that results from
interarea differences in effective tax rates. If differences in business property tax
levels between communities are matched by differences in the quantity and quality of public services supplied to business, then there is no problem. But this is
rarely the case. In most states property taxes go primarily to support schools.
Whatever one may estimate to be the benefit business receives from education in
the form of a more productive work force, it is difficult to argue that these benefits vary in a fashion even remotely resembling the wide variations in property
tax levels, even among closely neighboring communities. I can only conclude
that business property tax differentials among local areas are one of the major
nonneutralities associated with the property tax. The problem, I should note, is
not inherent in the tax itself but stems rather from the financing of such functions as schools through local levies on a geographically fragmented property tax
base.

Corporation Net Income Tax

Second to the property tax in dollar impact on business are state and local taxes
on corporate net income. The 1967 comparisons published by ACIR estimate
collections under such taxes at $2.5 billion, or 14 percent of the $17.9 billion in
taxes with an initial impact on business. Despite the fact that all but ten states
used some form of corporate net income tax in 1967 at either the state or local
level, or both, total impact on business was less than a fourth that of the property tax.

Economic theory suggests that a tax on business profits would be highly neutral if the tax were so designed as to fall on what in economics is termed "pure"
profit. Pure profit is that return over and above what is necessary to bring all
factors of production into use. If labor, landowners, owners of capital, and management were all rewarded at their going market price, any remaining income
would be pure profit, attributable to fortuitous circumstances or to a market
position characterized by some degree of monopoly. Pure profit, so defined,
would be limited and fairly transitory. Yet it could be taxed heavily without
causing withdrawal of the factors.

Of course, state and local taxes on corporation net income, like the federal
tax, are not confined to pure profit. The Internal Revenue Service concept of
net profit, like the accounting concept on which it is based, includes as profit
much that the economist would regard as return to capital and management, and

to a lesser extent land rent and wages. To the extent that it rests on these returns, the corporate net income tax discourages employment of the taxed factors. Studies of corporation income taxes suggest that the tax in fact is largely a charge against the return to capital and management, and as such is nonneutral among factors of production.

A second source of nonneutrality stems from the usual application of these taxes to corporations but not to unincorporated business. This discrimination is defended on the ground that government provides corporations with services and protections that are not available to the unincorporated business. The limited liability privilege is often cited. Even if this argument is accepted, a levy against net income would seem to be a crude way of recovering the added governmental cost, with many corporations being overcharged, and many others undercharged.

Sales Taxes

The only other business tax on which I shall comment is the general sales tax. The sales tax has certain well recognized distorting tendencies as it applies to consumers. It favors saving as against consumption, and nontaxed forms of consumption (notably personal services) as against purchase of commodities. Less well recognized are the nonneutralities of the retail sales tax in its direct impact on businesss, perhaps because of ambiguity in the nature of the sales tax.

Though seldom classed as a business tax, the sales tax applies to many business purchases. It is estimated that 15-25 percent of the average state's sales tax collections originate in the business sector. If this is so, it would appear that business pays somewhere between $2.0 and $3.5 billion annually in general sales tax—an amount of the same order of magnitude as that of state corporation net income taxes.

If we adopt the traditional textbook concept of the sales tax as a single-stage tax on consumption, then it is a mistake—a departure from neutrality—to include any business purchases in the tax base. To do so is to add a second layer of tax on those goods that require taxed inputs for their production. This viewpoint leads to the conclusion that all businesss purchases—raw materials, physical ingredients, machinery and equipment, office supplies, and so on—should be exempt.

But there is another conception of the sales tax that seems to me to conform more closely to the actual practice of sales tax states. This conceives the sales tax as a single-stage tax on all private purchases of final products. Viewed this way the sales tax, to be neutral, should be levied on business purchases of final products the same as on consumer purchases. Only nonfinal products would escape. In this form, the sales tax seems to me to resemble closely the value-added tax of the "gross product" type—in common with the value-added tax it would tax all final products uniformly, thereby scoring high on neutrality. Unlike the value-added tax, however, it is levied at the final stage only, and allows for certain classes of exempt purchasers, such as government. This latter concept of the sales tax suggests that the tax could be made more neutral if all business purchases other than intermediate products were subjected to sales tax.

Significance of State-Local
Business Tax Nonneutralities

Other discriminatory features of state and local business taxes could be mentioned, but those I have discussed are probably the most important in terms of the dollar amounts of tax involved and the probable magnitude of their distortions in market processes. Still, one may question how significant the nonneutralities tracing to state-local business taxes are in the total business decision-making process. I know of no good way to make quantitative estimates, but that should not deter us from speculating on the question.

First, let us remember that, for profitable firms—and thanks to loss carryovers and the market for tax-loss firms, for many unprofitable firms also—the impact of state and local taxes is cut roughly in half by the federal corporation income tax. Tax differentials likewise are halved. Whatever differentials there may be between the tax cost of building or not building, adding labor-saving equipment or not doing so, or locating a plant in one area rather than another, all are cut in half by the federal tax.

Probably the most widely recognized form of tax unneutrality is the differential among possible business locations. Businessmen are keenly aware of the tax consequences of locational choices. Politicians too are aware of the locational consequences of tax decisions. In my home state of Ohio I sometimes have the feeling that the makers of tax policy operate on the basis of only one rule—that low taxes attract business.

But a growing body of opinion and evidence seems to suggest that the influence of taxation on business location is less pronounced than formerly, or than we formerly thought. The findings of the ACIR study *State-Local Taxation and Industrial Location* generally discounted the significances of interstate tax differentials. Within states, and particularly within a single metropolitan area, the conclusion was that tax differentials are more likely to become the determining factor in locational choices. Even here I believe we are in danger of exaggerating the tax influence. Data assembled by my colleague, Professor Helen Cameron, indicate, for example, that the property tax consequences of the decision to locate in the lowest tax jurisdiction in the Columbus, Ohio, Standard Metropolitan Statistical Area rather than in the highest would make a difference of from well under 1 percent of operating costs to slightly more than 1 percent for the various kinds of businesses she studied. The range in property tax rates within the SMSA was about 2:1. A more disparate situation, such as the 3:1 range found in the Cleveland SMSA, would entail correspondingly greater tax consequences. And for individual firms the differences might of course be considerably greater.

Perhaps more important are nonneutralities among industries. Here again the property tax appears to be the main offender, discriminating against capital-intensive industries. Broadly speaking, manufacturing and public utilities are probably hardest hit. Service industries are less vulnerable. The way in which we finance state and local governments thus tends to impede development of industries that require heavy investment in capital. The strength of this tendency and its quantitative effects unfortunately cannot be readily estimated.

Tax Policies to Reduce Nonneutralities

If I am correct in my appraisal of the sources of nonneutrality in state-local business taxation and of their significance, it would follow that policies to reduce tax interferences with the working of the market system might appropriately focus on the property tax. This seems to be where the potential harm is greatest.

The radical solution, in the literal sense of getting to the root of the problem, would be to remove the tax from all reproducible property—tangible and intangible property, plus improvements to real estate—thereby converting our familiar property tax into a site value tax. As is well known, such a tax is about as neutral in terms of its allocative effects as any tax can be.

Short of this fundamental reform, some reduction in the economic distortions caused by the property tax could result from improving the accuracy of assessment, reducing geographic disparities in tax rates, avoiding piecemeal adjustments in the tax base (such as exemptions for farm personal property or commercial motor vehicles), and gradually reducing overall dependence on the property tax for state-local revenues. More extensive reliance on user charges at the local level would incorporate costs of governmental services more accurately into business costs of production, thereby advancing economic efficiency and at the same time reducing dependence on property taxes.

Greater neutrality could be achieved by certain other changes in a state-local tax system. The corporate net income tax, as has been noted, is less neutral as it applies to factor inputs than is the value-added tax alternative, though other considerations besides neutrality might well outweigh this advantage. Likewise a more neutral sales tax structure would result from applying the tax to all business purchases of final products.

One additional comment needs to be made concerning a deliberately non-neutral form of taxation that is receiving growing attention. I referred earlier to the use of taxation to increase the cost of activities that cause environmental pollution. The objective here is to impose on the producer a tax cost that matches as accurately as possible the social costs of his product—costs that under the market system cannot be brought into the production-consumption decision process. Here is a case where the market does not tend to produce a proper balance between costs and benefits, and where the general rule of neutrality gives way to the deliberate nonneutral use of taxes in such a way as to offset and correct for market imperfections. Perhaps the federal government is the proper unit to pursue this particular market-correcting use of taxation, but for state governments that are anxious to deal constructively and effectively with environmental problems this form of taxation seems worth considering.

Summary and Conclusion

Economics is concerned with how we use resources to the maximum benefit of all members of society. It informs us, in connection with state and local tax policy, that random, capricious interferences with the market system, are, on balance, likely to leave us worse off. We do well to scrutinize state-local tax policy to detect these interferences, to weigh their importance, and where possible to moderate or eliminate them. At the same time we need to remember that taxation can occasionally advance the welfare of society through constructive intervention in imperfect market processes. And finally we need to bear in mind constantly, especially those of us who call ourselves economists, that the economic consequences of tax policy are but one of many considerations that enter into the tax policy-making process.

Notes

1. Advisory Commission on Intergovernmental Relations, *Estimates of State and Local Taxes Initially Paid by Business Firms, 1957-1962-1967* (September, 1970), updating estimates published in *State-Local Taxation and Industrial Location* (A-30, April, 1967).

5

Discussion of Business Tax Components of a High Quality Tax System

Chairman Lewis C. Bell, *West Virginia University:* I think it is evident that the economist's viewpoint is a good one to have to round out a topic of this nature. I am not going to attempt to summarize what has gone forth this morning. For one reason it would take some doing, but primarily because we want to utilize the time now for questions and answers.

Dr. Lloyd E. Slater, *New York State Deputy Commissioner for Tax Research:* There have been many interesting things that I thought of as you went along, Professor Stocker. One thing that intrigued me was your use of the term tax for a charge in relation to pollutants in air and water by manufacturers. Although I know that others have used this same term of a tax, I am curious why you called it a tax instead of a service charge. You suggested a little earlier the use of service charges—you got pretty close to it—instead of taxes. Why do you term this a tax instead of a service charge?

Professor Frederick D. Stocker, *The Ohio State University:* I think you are probably right, Lloyd, in classifying a pollution charge as a service charge rather than as a tax.

Dr. Slater: The president didn't point it out that way, though. He called it a tax. Maybe somebody should change his mind.

Mr. Arnold Cantor, *AFL-CIO:* I wonder if we could get some comments on the role of the corporate income tax in raising revenue at the state and local levels.

Dr. John Shannon, *Advisory Commission on Intergovernmental Relations:* The Advisory Commission, while it has come down very hard on the need for effective state use of the personal income tax, has not come out directly and recommended equal treatment for corporate income. I do not, however, interpret that silence as necessarily indicating that our Commission would be against a corporate income tax. Far from it. It is just that it has not specifically faced this particular issue.

However, any of us who have tried to sell state legislative bodies on the need for a personal income tax know that if they moved in that direction—if they adopted one—it is almost certain that at the same time they would put a tax on corporations. If a person took a position that you should tax the income of individuals but not of corporations, the chances of enactment of a state personal income tax would be that much more difficult. Speaking from my own view, from a very pragmatic one, if the only way that I could facilitate more effective state use of the personal income tax would be to go along also with some type of a moderate tax on corporate income, I would go along with it.

I think there is a danger—I am trying to find a middle path here. Some of the public finance students take an extreme position that states and local governments have no business taxing business; that from the standpoint of neutrality and so on, business taxation should be the exclusive province of the federal government. On the other hand, we have extreme views on the other side, pragmatic politicians who say: Hit the business firm, especially the one with low mobility, for all you can get.

I believe you have to seek a middle ground, but my own predilection is to favor a tax on corporate income, especially if it is necessary to purchase sufficient public support in the legislative body for a personal income tax. Also, it is necessary in some cases in order to get support for removal of a much more mischievous tax, such as the personal property tax on business inventories. If that price is greater emphasis on the corporate income tax, again I would be willing to pay it.

Mr. Gary R. Mallory, *National Cash Register Company:* Our biggest concern is the property tax. In Wisconsin we went up to debate the assessment, and we found that on Mondays the local grocer was the tax assessor, and on the other six days a week he was the grocer. So a number of the gentlemen suggested that we have the state be the controlling board on this. They will assess all these different localities, and I agree with this.

Also, in Ohio we are having these outdoor recreation activities which are being taxed greatly. There was a reassessment of property taxes this year in Ohio, and in the Cincinnati district in a number of the country clubs assessments went up from 300 to 600 percent. About four or five counties followed this. The country clubs are not agreeing with this, and it is being debated right now. The concern is that the golf courses were being taxed at this rate, but they are in business for only about five or six months out of the year. This is not an equal distribution of taxes.

The reason that National Cash Register was brought into this is that we have country clubs along with other larger corporations, and if we have to increase our membership dues to meet this increase in taxes, this is going to cause a decline in golf, we fear. The whole point is that I think there should be something done with this property tax in that it is not equitable among different individuals.

Chairman Bell: All right. You were not asking anybody to respond?

Mr. Mallory: The only thing I wanted to comment on was that I am glad to see that there is a trend away from local assessment to state assessment.

Mr. Sidney Glaser, *New Jersey Division of Taxation:* I would like to comment on that. The mere fact that the tax is going up 300 percent is not indicative of its unfairness. They might have been assessed too low beforehand.

Mr. Richard E. Maine, *City of Baltimore Department of Finance:* ACIR recommends that state and local income taxes use the federal base (at least up to federal adjusted gross income) in order to simplify administration and produce substantial revenues.

Fifty weeks ago we heard Professor Stanley Surrey describe how the federal income tax, despite its progressive rates, produces many "regressive" effects and reduces its revenue potential through a variety of tax preference mechanisms. A state or local government wanting to correct or prevent some of these inequities by changes in adjusted gross income would further complicate the administration. Is it an advantage to have a uniformly bad base?

Dr. Shannon: First of all, I don't hope to be the expert on the federal tax code that Professor Surrey is. However, he was trying to paint a very somber picture of loopholes in the federal tax in order to try to hurry tax reform history along. The real question, I think, is to try to find a middle path. On the one hand, we want a tax that is as equitable as possible. On the other hand, this matter of taxpayer convenience—especially if state and perhaps local governments are using this same source—becomes of more and more concern.

I have noticed that the states that have recently enacted income taxes, especially since 1950, have moved far down the conformity path, and again apparently to minimize the amount of inconvenience for taxpayers. Nebraska for all practical purposes takes 10 percent or 12 percent of the federal tax as its tax. They go far beyond adjusted gross income. So do some of the others.

Again, I think that if I have to err on this, I would err on the side of conformity and promote taxpayer convenience, notwithstanding the fact that the Congress does not dot all its tax equity *i*'s and cross all its *t*'s as far as the treatment of capital gains and some of the other things are concerned.

Dr. Ronald B. Welch, *California State Board of Equalization:* I have a question I would like to direct to Dr. Shannon, and perhaps to Mr. Luckett if he cares to comment on it.

It relates to the credit against the income tax for sales tax payments on food or other necessities, and rebates in cases where there is not enough income tax liability to absorb the credit. You are aware of the chaos that is alleged to have arisen in Massachusetts, and also the fact that Iowa abandoned this device. I wonder if you would care to comment upon its practicability.

Mr. James E. Luckett, *Commissioner, Kentucky Department of Revenue:* Ron, if you included me just because you might feel that I was neglected, you didn't have to. I am aware that in many of the discussions there have been the two alternatives, either outright exemption of food or the credit, and John Shannon mentioned both of those. But I might be alone to the extent that I think there may possibly be a third choice, and that is one that I mentioned. That is dealing with the problem directly.

There is much talk about regressivity in the tax program, and I am glad to hear John leaning toward simplicity and taxpayer convenience. The need for simplicity and convenience is a serious problem because many of these credits can become rather complex for many people. You are involving two sets of taxes; the credit for sales tax against the income tax. Many people may not be capable of dealing with that problem. So my answer would be that I might lean very strongly toward a third solution. That is, deal with it as a direct program, as I indicated, rather than involving it in, and thereby increasing the complexities of, some other tax program.

Dr. Shannon: In defense of the credit, let me say that there is the simple credit, and then there is the more complicated diminishing credit. The simple credit is just a flat credit—each individual is given so much based on a calculated presumption of food tax payment. I don't believe that those states that use this straight flat credit for everybody find this a great problem, nor the rebate for those whose liability is so small or nonexistent that a refund is necessary.

Where the static apparently comes in is in pushing that concept a little bit farther and going to a diminishing credit, one that phases off as income rises. Iowa had that type. Massachusetts had a variant of this, and I think it was perhaps a combination of trying to convert the so-called regressive levy into a progressive tax to "make a silk purse out of a sow's ear" that overburdened the machinery. Not that the machinery couldn't be strengthened to handle that.

I don't think we should leave the impression that the flat rate credit creates great inconvenience. Moreover, the inconvenience that it creates for the tax administrator is more than offset by the convenience for the merchant who no longer has to keep two rolls of tapes on taxable and nontaxable items.

Professor John F. Due, *University of Illinois:* I would like to say something about the state experience. From my discussions with the tax administrators in various states that have the system, it appears in general to have worked very well. Massachusetts is an exception. The Massachusetts provision was defective in many ways. So was the provision in Iowa, and it became a political football. One party became committed to its repeal because of defects in it and proceeded to carry through the repeal. The Iowa administrator regarded the credit as entirely workable even though it was a graduated credit. I know in Colorado and Vermont, for instance, the administrators regarded the credit as entirely satisfactory.

Mr. Leonard E. Kust, *Cadwalader, Wickersham & Taft, New York:* I would like to direct a question to Professor Stocker. In your closing comments, you suggested that the sales tax might be made more neutral and comparable to the value-added tax if it were applied to all ultimate purchases by business as well as consumer purchases.

I am troubled by this because it seems to me that that would not make the two taxes comparable. There are two variants of the value-added tax which specifically allow either a deduction for all capital purchases from the value-added tax base, or, in the alternative, allow a depreciation allowance, so it seems to me that the value-added tax base does not include purchases of capital equipment consumed in production.

Secondly, it seems to me that if business purchases are included in a sales tax, to that extent you are introducing a pyramiding into the sales tax, because of necessity the capital purchases subjected to the sales tax will become a cost of production including the tax which will then presumably be included in the price of the ultimate product sold, resulting in a pyramiding of the tax.

Would you comment on these points, please?

Professor Stocker: I agree with your first point that the value-added tax, as it is usually conceived, does not include capital purchases but allows for an exemption of capital purchases or deduction for depreciation. Both the income type of value-added tax and the consumption type of value-added tax provide, though in different ways, for excluding capital purchases from the tax base. What I was referring to was a third type which has been defined or described as a gross product type of value-added tax, and I see no obvious reason why that type of tax might not be employed. Such a tax would, as you suggest, impose a tax on capital which would in turn raise the cost of production. Perhaps the final cost to the consumer would rise by more than the amount of the tax. But this problem is quite distinct from the usual pyramiding situation, which involves the same item being sold and resold through the production or distribution process.

I don't want to pose as an advocate of such a tax, but as I look at this matter of taxing business purchases, it seems to me that we would restore neutrality to our sales tax if we moved in the direction of more comprehensive coverage of business purchases of final products rather than less.

Mr. James A. Jacobs, *Southern Bell Telephone & Telegraph Company:* I guess this would be for comment by Professor Stocker too. It seems to me that in the discussions today there are two points of interest that haven't been alluded to.

The first is the question of business taxation. If you assume, as Professor Stocker suggested, that additional costs on business are ultimately going to be reflected in the cost of the product or service that they produce, how should business taxes be influenced by the regressivity on the ultimate consumer of their services? That is, who pays the taxes finally? Should we give some consideration to where that ultimate impact comes and whether or not one tax is more regressive ultimately than another?

The second is a totally different thing. What about the states that are able to, or make efforts to, pass their cost of government on to residents of other states through taxes on their products? The most evident are the severance taxes, in the states which are heavy producers of gas and oil, that raise the price of gas and oil all over the United States, but lower the taxes on the citizens of those states. Should that not be given some consideration in business taxes?

Professor Stocker: You ask should we not be concerned, in designing the business tax structure, with the distributional characteristics of the tax. Right? My opinion is that we ought not to be greatly concerned with regressivity or progressivity in distribution of the incidence of business taxes. From the standpoint of the economist, it seems to me we ought to be concerned with neutrality. If we want to correct the income distribution, we ought to resort to other more direct methods through direct taxes on income or through direct payments to people whose incomes are too low. So if I understood your question, my own feeling is that this is not an important consideration in business taxation.

On this matter of severance taxation, I hate to duck, but I think I really ought not to attempt to comment. There is so much that would have to be said, that I don't think I ought to embark on it at this late stage in the session.

Mr. Allen D. Manvel, *Advisory Commission on Intergovernmental Relations:* This is really a postscript to that question. I wonder if you might accept as an adjustment of your reactions that you were pretty much talking about business taxes in a broad sense, those taxes in relation to their hitting of business generally. Wouldn't you accept as a modification that we actually do have many, or some, tax instruments used by state and local governments that target at particular kinds of business? One can think especially of targeting at utilities or railroads. Severance taxes are another example.

Now as soon as one moves away from the broader taxes to that kind of thing, then it seems to me that some of these incidents and distributional effects are surely unneutral potentially in the first instance, and that worries you and would worry me. I am concerned with it from that standpoint. Isn't there at that stage much more of a possible concern about potential distributional effects as such?

Professor Stocker: Income distribution?

Mr. Manvel: Yes, and impact as to the kinds of economic activity that are going to be carried on.

Professor Stocker: I suppose you are thinking of public utility taxes which tend to be highly regressive.

Mr. Manvel: That is right.

Professor Stocker: No, I would stand by what I said before. I think it is important to recognize the income distribution consequences of state business taxation, but I don't believe that we can do much through state and local taxation, or adjustments thereto, to correct what might be a faulty or undesirable distribution of income.

Again, I had it in mind to comment in my paper generally on this point of the business taxes that single out an industry—insurance companies, financial institutions, public utilities—and make the point that I think you made, Allen, that these are a prominent source of nonneutrality in our tax system. But their effects on income distribution, it seems to me, should not be a major element in policy making at the state and local level.

Dr. Slater: May I raise this question in a different form? I personally am inclined to agree with Professor Stocker that once you have settled on a level of business taxation it should be applied in a way to be as neutral as possible among the factors of production. Perhaps, though, the point that is being raised does have some relevance to the amount of total tax burden that should be assessed on business rather than being assessed more directly on individuals.

It has seemed to me more and more in recent years, particularly in order to be successful at all in our state and local business taxes, that they must of necessity be the type of tax that can be passed on. If you can accomplish that, if you can make all the competitors pay the same tax, regardless of the level of the state and local taxes you have, it is not a burden on the business. Then it is just something they become a collector for. Your only problem of a burden on business is created in a situation where some competitors can avoid the tax, and then even a very low rate of tax that would have to be absorbed by the business could be so burdensome that the business eventually declines and moves somewhere else. It does seem to me that for the most part you have to have state and local taxes that business can pass forward. To the extent that you decide to collect your total state and local revenue from business enterprises and let them pass this revenue through, it probably is a more regressive method of collecting your taxes than we usually try to impose in our direct taxation of individuals.

Mr. Robert Kleine, *Michigan Budget Division:* I have a two-part question. In Michigan in about 1967 we had a business activities tax replaced by the corporate income tax. First, the business activity tax based on sales activity is more stable, not quite as involved as the corporate income tax, but the question is: What would the attitudes of the members of the panel be to the differences between the business activities tax and the corporate income tax, and also what is the attitude toward another criterion for taxes which wasn't mentioned, but which from a practical standpoint I think is important, the stability of the tax. I think this has implications for expenditure policies. Having taxes fluctuate up and down makes it difficult to keep expenditures and revenue in balance. I was wondering if any of the panel would make a comment on these questions.

Professor Stocker: I think I suggested in my remarks that the value-added tax, if it is properly designed—and I think your problems in Michigan were with the design of the tax—would be preferable from the standpoint of neutrality to the conventional, corporate net income tax. Problems of administration might outweigh this, but speaking strictly from the standpoint of economic effects, it seems to me this is a very desirable form of taxation, although I know it is a subject on which informed opinions differ.

Professor C. Lowell Harriss, *Columbia University:* One of the characteristics that might be considered in evaluating the tax system, about which relatively little has been said this morning, is tax consciousness, the relationship between the tax paid and the awareness, and, therefore, the growth of government expenditures at the state and local level as well as the national level. One event of the last few years—and it seems to me it will continue in the foreseeable future—is considerable upward pressure for more and more spending. Now, are we getting our money's worth for this spending in this long-range problem?

Another question is: Does the public that is voting for the expenditures and exerting pressure for them, realize that someone is going to have to pay for them? And, so far as business taxes are concerned, is not one of the attractions of business taxes, to some people, the fact that businesses don't vote—the fact that you can have taxation without representation to a considerable degree. Therefore, if tax consciousness, or the connection between the evaluation of the worth of expenditures and the expectation of who is to pay for them are properly related, then the indirect taxes collected through the business organizations, need to be reexamined in this light.

I think John Shannon is perfectly correct in saying that the price we pay for a personal income tax is a tax on corporation earnings yet the two are not the same in their economic effects and in their incidence. Although the public official facing this problem has to accept this price, we might, at least in a discussion such as this, very well recognize the fact that taxes on corporation income are not the same as taxes on personal income.

Part II: Policy Implications of the Quantitative Distribution of Tax Burden Between Business and Nonbusiness Taxes

The opening session of the symposium identified and weighed the characteristics of a high quality state and local tax system and its business tax components.

At this session we shall turn our attention to the policy implications of the quantitative distribution of the tax burden between business and nonbusiness taxes. We will try to determine whether the present quantitative distribution is consistent with those characteristics of a high quality tax system that were outlined this morning. With this task of evaluating the present distribution of the tax burden between business and nonbusiness taxpayers, let us proceed and see where our efforts will take us.

Arthur P. Becker

Professor of Economics, University of Wisconsin-Milwaukee, and Chairman of Thursday Afternoon Session

6

Identification of Business and Nonbusiness State and Local Taxes and Its Policy Implications

John F. Due

The field of taxation labeled "taxes on business" or "business taxes" is characterized, more than any other area of taxation, by confusion in terminology, failure to establish objectives, lack of rationale in policy, obscurity in analysis, lack of knowledge of and concern for distributional effects, and some deliberate effort on the part of governments to conceal realities from the public. This paper seeks to clarify terminology and to consider the question of identification of state and local business taxes and its significance for policy.

Taxes on Business

In the broadest sense, the term "taxes on business" may be used for levies under which business firms, as distinct from individuals not engaged in business, are involved in any way. There are several categories:

I. Taxes paid by business firms directly to governments, without explicit or implicit instructions that the amounts be collected by the firms from anyone else. There are two subclasses:
    A. General levies that apply both to businesses and individuals. The property tax is the prime example, but the portion of the personal income tax applying to noncorporate incomes may be included as well.
    B. Levies applied specifically to businesses, per se, or to major categories of business, such as corporations:
        1. Corporation income taxes.
        2. Gross receipts business taxes, such as the West Virginia and Washington business and occupation taxes, and portions of the Hawaii general excise tax structure.
        3. Value-added taxes, as used for a time in Michigan and proposed for other states.
        4. Capital stock taxes.
        5. License charges, state and local, whether based on gross receipts or other criteria, or flat amounts for particular occupations.
        6. Levies on particular types of business, such as severance taxes and taxes on insurance companies. Motor vehicle levies will be excluded

57

from this discussion as a part of the user fee system for highway finance.

II. Taxes paid by business firms to vendors who are explicitly or implicitly expected to collect the taxes from the purchasers, business or individual. The major example is the portion of the retail sales tax applying to purchases for business use, estimated to be from 15 percent to 25 percent or more of total sales tax collections.[1] The motor fuel levies, also of this character, are excluded from this discussion because of their user-charge nature.

III. Taxes paid to government by business firms that are regarded—usually explicitly by law but sometimes only implicitly—as tax collecting agents for government, since they are required or expected to reimburse themselves from other persons. The principal example is the retail sales tax; in fact in Canada the vendors are designated by law as tax collecting agents. The portion of the income tax that employers are required to withhold from wages paid employees is also of this character.

IV. Other taxes that may be shifted to business firms. These include various taxes in I.B. above that are shifted from the initial business firm to another, the personal income tax on employees to the extent that it is shifted to the employer in higher wages, and the retail sales tax on consumer goods, to the extent that it is reflected in higher wages.

The exhaustiveness of this list suggests that if the concept of "taxes on business" and the percentage of total tax revenue consisting of "taxes on business" are to be of any significance some of the levies noted must be eliminated from the category. But there is no obvious, self-evident guide for doing so on the basis of the external character of these taxes alone. The Advisory Commission on Intergovernmental Relations (ACIR) includes in its classification of business taxes only those in category I.B. above—the specific levies on business—plus the portion of the property tax on business property (portion of I.A. above).[2] ACIR notes the existence of sales taxes on business purchases but excludes them on the grounds that they are "primarily direct consumer levies." This is of little consolation to the firms that have to pay them. But it is obvious that this is only one possible approach. Appropriate classification requires more detailed analysis of the effects of these various taxes on the firms and their distributional impact. Only a brief review is possible in this paper.

Effects of the Various Types of Taxes

The Property Tax

By far the largest single element in the ACIR tabulation is the portion of the property tax imposed directly on business property—$10 billion out of $18 billion total taxes on business under the ACIR concept in 1967. A portion of the property tax may be regarded as an appropriate application of the benefit or user-charge principle, placing the costs of police and fire protection, street lighting, and other services for which property is directly responsible upon the businesses benefiting from and necessitating these services. Ultimately this tax element, like any other cost element for necessary resources, will be reflected in the prices of the products; this may be regarded as appropriate since these elements are compensations for real economic costs incurred in the production of the goods and do not constitute a burden on business that is harmful to it or in any way objectionable.

A large portion of the property tax, however, is used to finance education, and other elements finance welfare, health, and other functions not related to property ownership. In part this tax is undoubtedly reflected in higher prices for the products of the businesses. But this shifting is likely to be very imperfect and uneven, as the ratios of tax to sales vary widely. The property-intensive types of production will suffer permanent loss in business. Netzer's study indicates that the railroad industry is most adversely affected, because it competes with forms of transport with relatively little taxable property relative to receipts.[3] The effect is increased by deliberate overvaluation of railroad property in some states. Netzer's work as well as that of others also concludes that the part of the property tax resting on business inventories has more significant effects on firms and in altering location decisions than real property taxes.[4] A state that taxes inventories and has relatively high property tax rates will almost certainly lose fabrication and wholesale distribution activity to nearby states.

State Corporation Income Taxes

While our knowledge of the shifting and distributional effects of corporate income taxes is far from perfect, there is reason to believe that a substantial portion rests upon the owners of the business firms, thus giving the states some claim on the earnings of firms doing business in the state and benefiting from overall state services, and complementing, though not perfectly, the state personal income taxes. So long as the corporate income tax in a state is reasonably comparable to those of other states and to the personal income tax, there is no reason to believe that the tax has significant effects on locational decisions. Obviously the owners of the business experience a reduction in real income—but so do all other income receivers under a tax system substantially related to income. Only when the corporate rate gets to 10 percent or so, with 5 to 7 percent the typical figures, does there appear to be any significant danger to the business firm and to the economy of the state.

Gross Receipts Taxes

Fortunately gross receipts business taxes are neither very widespread nor high in rate. But where they exist they may have substantial impact on many business firms, because of the difficulty of shifting them when competing firms in other states are not subject to comparable levies. Even a 1 percent tax on gross receipts may have disastrous effects on relatively unprofitable firms when they cannot raise prices to compensate for them. The taxes likewise have potentially adverse effects on firms in nonintegrated distribution systems compared to integrated firms and therefore encourage integration, in the same fashion as national turn-over taxes do. To the extent that the taxes do shift, the firms may escape burden, but the final distributional impact on individuals will be haphazard and uneven compared to that of a retail sales tax, since ratios of tax to final retail selling prices will vary.

Some of these considerations apply to a value-added tax at the state level; incentive to integrate is avoided, but some firms may have difficulty in shifting all of the tax forward in the absence of effective means of taxing goods coming in from other states. On a national basis a value-added tax is essentially equivalent to a retail sales tax and should be evaluated accordingly.

Capital Stock and License Taxes

These, if at any magnitude at all, are particularly injurious to business firms since the ratios of tax to sales will vary widely among different firms, thus making shifting difficult and placing a serious burden on the high-tax firms.

Levies on Particular Types of Business

These can be evaluated only in terms of the nature of the particular levy and the type of business involved. To include severance taxes in statewide comparisons of relative magnitudes of "taxes on business," however, is misleading, since their potential applicability in various states is so different and the effect on particular extractive industries varies with the nature of the markets for the products. Two states, Texas and Louisiana, collect nearly 80 percent of the total severance tax revenue in the United States.

The Sales Tax on Business Purchases

These total about $1.3 billion, according to ACIR estimates updated to 1970; under other estimates they would be as high as $1.8 billion. The states differ widely in their policies. The largest group of states, 19, confine the exclusion of producers' goods to sales for resale, sales of materials becoming physical ingredients, and farm feed, seed, and fertilizer.[a] Three additional states add to the exemption some goods consumed in the industrial process and industrial fuel. Fourteen states exclude industrial machinery and equipment, three exempt machinery used for expansion of industry, and six tax machinery at a lower rate. Ohio excludes most items used in industry, agriculture, and retailing (not wholesaling), and West Virginia excludes virtually all purchases for production use.

The net effect of taxing various producers' goods is to place an additional tax burden on the owners of those businesses unable to shift all of the tax because of market conditions, particularly because of the failure of competing industrial states to tax these goods. New York, Pennsylvania, Ohio, Michigan, Indiana, West Virginia, and in part Kentucky, exempt industrial machinery, for example; Illinois and New Jersey do not. The result is some discrimination against industry in the last two states and therefore some adverse effects on locational decision making. Even with shifting, total investment may be reduced as more money capital is needed; incentive is given to use less capital-intensive methods, and the final distribution of tax on consumers is uneven and haphazard, depending on their relative preferences for goods that have large elements of cost of taxable goods in the final selling prices. At the early 2 percent sales tax rates, the effects may have been negligible; at 5 and 6 percent rates the effects become more serious; at possible future 8 or 10 percent rates the effects may be little short of disastrous.

Business Firms as Tax Collectors

Taxes for which vendors serve as collecting agents are typically not regarded as taxes on business firms under the assumption that they have no effect on the firms. Clearly this is not so. State and local sales taxes cost the retailer money to collect—added time of clerks, time for ascertaining tax liability and making out tax returns, and possibly more expensive cash register equipment. The amounts involved are difficult to ascertain, and some estimates are suspect. The information required is the increase in total expense resulting from the existence of the tax and this is not easily calculated. Multiplying the time taken by the clerks in adding the tax at the cash register by the average wage does not give an accurate measure, because the idle time clerks might otherwise have is not taken into consideration. The estimate by J.L. Fisher of the J.C. Penney Company that the typical cost is 2.5 percent (with a 4 percent tax rate) may be taken as a reasonable one.[5] Presumably this cost will ultimately be reflected in higher overhead markups and shifted to the consumers. But given retail pricing methods this may be a very slow process. Furthermore, the figure obviously varies widely among

[a]Hawaii does not exempt these sales but taxes most of them at a low (.5 percent) rate.

business firms, depending on the nature of the business, average size of transaction, etc. It is high for variety stores; it is almost negligible for car dealers. Because of the wide variation, the practice of some states of providing a vendor discount or compensation of 2 percent or so of the tax due overcompensates some and undercompensates others; it is more equitable to let the actual costs be reflected ultimately in higher markups.

Secondly, state and local sales taxes, because of their geographic nonuniformity, injure the firms located close to borders of jurisdictions having lower taxes, and locational decisions are affected. The Hamovitch study of New York City showed a significant (6 percent) loss in sales as a result of the New York City tax,[6] and the recent study by Mikesell shows substantial loss for those metropolitan centers having higher sales tax rates than surrounding areas.[7] Because of the tendency of sales to fall, firms may absorb the tax in part, particularly on larger items. In general, apart from the border problem, there is no assurance that all of the sales tax shifts forward to customers; the mere fact that a law says that vendors shall collect the tax from their customers does not ensure that they do so, since they may reduce prices net of tax, especially on larger items. Separate quotation requirements facilitate shifting by promoting uniformity of action among retailers, but they do not ensure it. Finally, to the extent that the taxes do shift, consumer reactions may be quite different on some goods than on others, even when all prices are rising, and thus producers of those products whose sales fall most sharply are adversely affected. All taxes—income and others—reduce sales; the reaction to sales taxes is likely to be somewhat different from that to other taxes.

As collectors of withholding taxes, business firms are likewise put to some expense in making deductions and remitting taxes due and are subjected to hazards of penalties for making mistakes. But more significantly, it is widely recognized that workers are more concerned about take-home pay than nominal total pay. The withholding tax influences unions in their demands and their settlement figures. The income tax almost certainly affects the bargaining with higher executives and skilled technicians. Thus the costs of the firms are increased. These increases are likely to shift forward, but by no means uniformly or perfectly. Sales taxes may have similar effects on wage rates.

This analysis, brief as it is, suggests that all of these taxes may have some adverse effects on business firms. There is no sharp, clear-cut line between levies that should be regarded as levies "on business" because they significantly affect business and those that do not. Certainly the retail sales tax on business purchases, excluded from the ACIR tabulation, has significant effects. Retail sales taxes on consumer goods are universally excluded from the class of "taxes on business" yet they may have relatively substantial effects. They are, after all, not very different from gross receipts business taxes which are universally included, and in fact are not legally distinguished from the other business taxes in the Hawaii general excise tax structure.

General Conclusions

In conclusion: this discussion suggests a few general observations.

1. Classification of taxes on the basis of whether they are "on business" or "not on business" and thus on individuals is a meaningless and dangerous exercise, as there is no possible scientific basis for drawing a significant line between the two categories.
2. Accordingly, figures of taxes "on business" published by ACIR or other sources are meaningless and have no significance for tax policy; there is no possible way of setting up a standard as to the appropriate percentages to come from each category.
3. The significant question about taxes affecting businesses is: what are the effects of a given state-local tax structure upon business firms in general and in particular industries? What significance do these effects have for economic development of the state and for desired distributional patterns? What changes would eliminate the evils? The worst offenders appear to be the part of the property tax on business firms, the state business and occupation taxes based on gross receipts, the portion of the sales tax applying to business purchases, and corporation income taxes far out of line with those of other states competitive for industry.
4. The confused and unascertainable distributional effects of certain business taxes suggest the need for minimizing reliance upon them, if desired distributional goals are to be attained. The property tax on business property (except for the benefit-related portion), the gross receipts and capital stock taxes, and the portion of the sales tax on producers' goods are the most obscure but are almost certainly the most haphazard in their distributional pattern.
5. The user-charge portion of the property tax, a corporation income tax not too far out of line with competitive states, the sales tax applying to consumer purchases, and, of course, the personal income tax, while not without some effects on business firms, appear to be the least objectionable levies affecting business, so far as adverse effects on business and economic development, economic distortions, and equity are concerned. The worst effect, in actual magnitude, appears to arise from the portion of the property tax affecting business inventories and the heavy burden on the railroads, which interferes with the attainment of an optimal transport system.

Despite their limitations, taxes on business, especially those with obscure distributional effects, have great political appeal. Many persons appear to regard a tax on business as a levy on the enterprise, per se, and thus not falling on any human beings who are voters. This is of course nonsense; any tax must reduce the real income of some individuals, and analysis of distributional effects without regard to the persons whose incomes are affected is meaningless. Corporations do not have taxpaying ability in and of themselves, but only as agents for people—owners, employees, customers, etc. Liberals seeking a higher portion of tax on the wealthy frequently favor business taxes as a means of attaining this objective—yet the objective is in all likelihood rarely attained by this means.

There are many examples of these tendencies. One of the most glaring is the common tendency to value business property more heavily than property of individuals, or, as in Arizona, to apply, by law, a heavier tax burden on railroads and other types of business property than on individual property. The 1970 proposed amendment to the Illinois constitution exempts personal property owned by individuals but not others. Two years ago, when the province of Ontario needed additional sales tax revenue, the tax was extended to industrial machinery—a politically attractive but economically undesirable approach. In Illinois a major issue over the income tax has been the relative rates of the individual and corporate taxes—with strong popular and particularly liberal support for a higher rate on corporations. There is no necessity, by any standard, that the two income taxes have the same rate. But a heavier levy on companies is not necessarily the most effective way of putting more burden on the wealthy. Heavier property taxes on business property and sales taxes on business purchases are certainly not effective ways of doing so, because of shifting of the taxes.

The way to make a tax structure progressive relative to income and wealth, an objective I fully support, is to rely primarily upon progressive income taxes on individuals with comparable taxes on corporate income, not to load burdens on businesses per se.

Notes

1. Richard F. Fryman, "Sales Taxation of Producers' Goods in Illinois," *National Tax Journal*, 22 (June, 1969), 273-81; Daniel C. Morgan, Jr., *Retail Sales Tax—An Appraisal of New Issues* (Madison: The University of Wisconsin Press, 1964), p. 14.

2. *State-Local Taxation and Industrial Location* (A-30, April, 1967).

3. Dick Netzer, *Economics of the Property Tax* (Washington, D.C.: The Brookings Institution, 1966), p. 73.

4. Ibid., p. 163.

5. J.L. Fisher, "How Much Does It Cost to Collect Sales Taxes?" *Proceedings of the . . . National Tax Association, 1961* (Harrisburg, 1962), pp. 619-24.

6. William Hamovitch, "Effects of Increases in Sales Tax Rates on Taxable Sales in New York City," in *Financing Government in New York City*, Final Research Report of the Graduate School of Public Administration, New York University, to the Temporary Commission on City Finances, City of New York (New York, 1966), pp. 619-33.

7. John L. Mikesell, "Central Cities and Sales Tax Rate Differentials: The Border City Problem," *National Tax Journal*, 23 (June, 1970), 206-13.

7

Interstate Business Tax Comparisons: Reflections on One State's Experience

John W. Ingram

The somewhat controversial subject of interstate business tax comparisons has been a common item on the agenda of most meetings such as this one, and has filled many pages of tax conference proceedings, textbooks, and periodicals. In view of the extensive, and sometimes studiously abstract, literature available on this subject, it might be appropriate to examine, against the background of actual problems and experience in one state, the approaches and the effectiveness of actual efforts to measure and compare interstate burdens of taxes on business and industry and to utilize the results.

For this purpose, I believe, Pennsylvania has unique qualifications as a laboratory specimen. Pennsylvania has a long history of taxing business. Its first statewide tax, enacted in 1814, was a 6 percent tax on bank dividends, followed twenty-six years later by a general corporate tax on capital stock. Exemption from that tax for manufacturers, introduced almost a century ago, gave early recognition to the policy of special tax devices to attract industry into the state. Throughout its history, Pennsylvania, as a heavily industrialized state, has exhibited a classic pattern of extraordinary and changeable reliance on business generally, and manufacturing in particular, as a primary source of state revenue.

The predictable result has been an exceptional number and variety of formal tax studies, differing in motivation and scope, but in most cases devoting special concern and attention to the measurement of business tax burdens and appraisal of their impact on the state's economic welfare.

With your indulgence, I shall summarize the methods employed and uses made of these studies, against the changing business tax environment which motivated them. Based on these experiences in Pennsylvania, some observations might be derived concerning the validity and usefulness of interstate business tax comparisons and some possibilities for improving them in the future.

1935 to 1955: A High Tax Plateau

The burden of business taxation does not seem to have been a major issue or cause of concern in Pennsylvania until the Depression-racked years of the 1930s. Although corporate taxes historically had been the state's principal tax breadwinners, apparently until the mid-1930s there was little interest in comparing Pennsylvania's business tax burdens with those in other states.

65

This evident lack of corporate tax concern presumably reflected the relatively innocuous revenue-raising pressures on the state level of government, and perhaps a somewhat more active concern by corporate taxpayers with locally imposed (and locally negotiable) property taxes.

This comparative state of relaxation was rudely shattered by the onset of the Great Depression. Faced with sudden and unprecedented demands for new social welfare and other Depression-spawned services, and with a corresponding upsurge of demands for expanded revenue sources, Pennsylvania in the mid-1930s sharply altered its state tax structure with a pronounced emphasis on industry as the prime producer. In a single legislative session, in 1935, aggregate corporate tax yields were more than doubled by enactment of a new tax on corporate net income, expansion of the base of the capital stock tax and removal of its special exemption for manufacturers, and increases in rates of other general and selective corporate taxes. At the same time, the state's first unemployment compensation tax was imposed.

The increased reliance by the state on corporation taxes was the product of a conscious policy decision which rejected the alternative of initiating broad-base taxes on either sales or personal income, such as were being adopted by other states faced with the same problem. This decision was fortified by the Pennsylvania Supreme Court's rejection, on constitutional grounds, of a personal income tax enacted in 1935.

The new Pennsylvania structure of high-level corporate taxes, although originally tagged as an "emergency" measure, established a pattern which persisted for two decades, and earned Pennsylvania an unenviable nationwide reputation as a "high business-tax" state.

Studies by the Dozen

The predictable reaction during the two high business-tax decades was a steady and prolific production of special tax or fiscal studies, numbering a dozen in all, and conducted under official or private sponsorship. These typically were charged with the partial or exclusive mission of investigating the relative burdens of taxes on business in Pennsylvania, and attempting to analyze their impact on the state's economic growth and welfare.[a]

The origin and sponsorship of the studies was equally distributed between business groups, the state legislature, and the governor. They demonstrated a wide variety of approaches and methods used to size up Pennsylvania's tax burdens, including those on business, against those imposed by other states.[b]

[a]A chronological listing of Pennsylvania tax study reports issued since 1925 is in Appendix A.

[b]Editor's Note: Also, Pennsylvania members of the Tax Institute of America (then Tax Institute, Incorporated), under the sponsorship of the Institute, conducted three conferences on Pennsylvania's tax problems during the 1950s. The proceedings were published by the Institute as follows: *The Pennsylvania Tax Question*, 1953, 144 pp.; *The Pennsylvania Tax Problem 1955*, 210 pp.; and *Pennsylvania Tax Problems in 1957*, 130 pp.

Total spending and tax trends were related to population, personal income, and various measures of investment and production, in order to compare overall tax burdens and their relationship to economic factors. The shares of total tax burden allocated to business and industry were compared, usually in terms of the percentage of total taxes collected from general or specific business sources. These were sometimes supplemented by descriptive comparisons of the various states' tax laws and their administrative features. Businessmen were queried as to the influence of high taxes on their relocation or expansion choices.

One of the earliest studies of the period, completed in 1938, introduced the "hypothetical corporation" method of computing and comparing tax liabilities of model corporations located in selected states. The principal advantage of this approach, despite its acknowledged difficulty, was that it permitted pinpointing and comparing tax liabilities of manufacturing corporations alone, which were a primary consideration and concern in Pennsylvania.

Perhaps the most exhaustive of the studies of that period was that undertaken by a governor-appointed committee headed by the late Dr. Alfred G. Buehler. This committee employed both the more conventional statistical measures and the hypothetical corporate model approaches for measuring total and industrial tax burdens, and comparing these with other selected industrial states. The conclusions of that committee, reported in 1953 and 1955, confirmed and were remarkably similar to those of almost a dozen previous tax studies. They found that Pennsylvania, in its industrial tax burden rankings, was at or near the top among competitive industrial states, and that in terms of its reliance on state business taxes, Pennsylvania outranked all other states, an unenviable position which was modified only by its relatively favorable local tax burdens on business and by its relatively low levels of total spending and tax collection.

The effectiveness of these early studies and their published findings, in terms of influencing state tax policy in the direction of reduced burdens on industry, might well be questioned in the light of the legislative record up through the mid-1950s.

During the period from 1935 to 1955 direct corporate tax collections rose from less than one-third to well over one-half of total state revenues. The rate of the so-called "emergency tax" on corporate income was increased four times, special corporation taxes were also increased, and the capital stock manufacturers exemption, although restored in 1937, had its effective date successively postponed for the following twenty years. A broad liberalization of local taxing discretion under Pennsylvania's unique "tax anything" law (Act 481), passed in 1947, provided some measure of relief from local property taxes on business enterprises. However, the state government, which persistently rejected adopting broad-based income or sales taxes as a means of financing its increasing revenue demands, was forced to increase rather than to reduce its reliance upon corporation taxes.

Despite these indications of the ineffectiveness of the tax studies, the combined and repeated expressions in these studies of alarm at the evidence of Pennsylvania's comparative overreliance on state taxes on industry, and the possible consequent risking of its proper share of industrial expansion, seemed to lead to a growing official embarrassment and a compelling awareness of this problem, and of the need for its correction. Unquestionably, these studies played a significant role in setting the stage for a shift in Pennsylvania toward aggressive pursuit of a favorable industrial tax climate which in subsequent years would improve its competitive capacity to attract new and expanded industry.

**Fifteen Years of Tax Climate
Improvement**

During the fifteen years from the mid-1950s until the past year, conscious and bipartisan joint efforts of public officials and of business, labor, and other economic interests, led to a remarkable shift of tax policy geared toward the development of a more attractive environment for the location of manufacturing industry in Pennsylvania. The focus on attracting manufacturers reflected the prominence of this segment of business enterprise as a prime investor, producer, and employer in Pennsylvania. It also recognized the relative mobility of manufacturers, and the economic reliance of utilities and financial and commercial enterprises upon manufacturing growth.

Implementation of this policy change was brought about through two primary courses of action. One was the shift of state revenue reliance to a broadbased consumer sales tax adopted on a permanent basis in 1956. This tax, with successive expansions of its base and increases in its rate, soon replaced corporation taxes as the state's primary income producer.

The second course of action was the restoration or introduction of tax exemptions and exclusions directed and limited to manufacturers, and granting them relief from the state sales and capital stock and franchise taxes and from local property taxes on machinery and equipment.

One measure of the results was that the ratio of direct corporation taxes to total state general purpose taxes, which had climbed to well over 50 percent in the mid-1950s, was returned back to the pre-1930s level of approximately 30 percent.

A New Breed of Tax Studies

During this period of improved business tax climate the volume of Pennsylvania tax studies and related state business tax burden comparisons did not abate as might have been anticipated. However, the objective of this later breed of studies was altered from attempting to measure the state's unfavorable tax posture and its deleterious effects on industrial development, to a new dual objective of, first, supporting administrative and legislative reform measures and, second, advertising their results for industrial development purposes. These objectives fostered new and more sophisticated interstate industrial tax burden comparisons, which were featured prominently in most of the eleven tax study reports issued since 1955.

The auspices under which the more recent tax studies were made also underwent change. No formal legislative-sponsored studies were carried out during the 1950s and 1960s. A new type of tax-study sponsor entered the picture, represented by industrial development agencies, public and private, who were anxious to capitalize on the new image of a favorable tax climate. Three governor-appointed citizen committees, each having a similar representation of top-echelon labor, business, university, and local government representatives, dominated the field of official state government tax investigations. The immediate mission of each was to discover sources of added revenue sufficient to cover impending budget deficits, while at the same time maintaining an equitable tax system which would not deter industrial growth and development. The most recent of these commissions, appointed in 1967, was charged with a further responsibility of recommending a plan for meeting the long-term revenue requirements of the state and its local governments.

Six consecutive interstate business tax comparison studies were made between 1956 and 1969 by the Pennsylvania Economy League, a private nonprofit research organization. The League studies were utilized by the State Department of Commerce, by regional industrial developers, and by successive governors' tax committees for the dual purpose of measuring and exploiting the state's improving business tax climate and for establishing tax policy guidelines.

There were two unique features of the Pennsylvania Economy League studies which deserve mention. One was that, as a series using common measuring bases and techniques, they provided a means of tracing the effect of sequential legislative or administrative tax policy actions on Pennsylvania's competitive tax climate. A second feature was that the studies combined a number of the most common methods of measuring and comparing among states the general burdens of state and local taxes, with hypothetical corporate-model methods of testing tax burdens on specific classes of manufacturing industry.

Traditional statistical measures of expenditure levels and total tax and debt burdens, related to population and personal income, were presented, along with descriptive comparisons of state tax sytems. Unemployment compensation systems were compared in terms of benefit and financing provisions. Tax liabilities computed for hypothetical manufacturing corporations included local as well as state taxes, and in one case included sewer and water charges. Local tax liabilities were computed on both a statewide average basis, and in selected actual locations.

The findings traced and confirmed the progressive improvements in Pennsylvania's industrial tax climate burden rankings among competing states, resulting from recurrent legislative tax relief measures enacted during the past fifteen years. They revealed that total state and local general tax levels were lower in Pennsylvania than in most comparable industrial states. Pennsylvania state taxes on most manufacturing enterprises, compared with those imposed by other states competing for industrial attraction, were found to have moderated from their former high-ranking positions, while local business taxes retained their favorable low-profile stature.

Effectiveness of Recent Studies

Difficult as it is to measure the effectiveness of any tax study, I believe that there is tangible evidence that the studies conducted since 1955 exerted a considerable influence upon both the initial change of policy which generated a substantial improvement in Pennsylvania's industrial tax posture, and in the subsequent maintaining of that policy up to the close of the past year. In large measure, this effectiveness was vastly enhanced by the three successive governor-appointed tax study committees, who utilized the comparative tax analysis results to support their tax climate improvement recommendations to the respective governors and through them to the legislature. Similar long-range recommendations presented in 1969 by the most recent committee, although carefully and widely considered, were overshadowed by political considerations when during the past year, Pennsylvania legislators had to face the equally hazardous political alternatives of reducing expenditures or adopting a politically unpopular personal income tax.

A resulting legislative impasse was resolved finally by turning to business taxes for the major share of the massive revenue increase required. The upward shift in tax burdens on business and industry was comparable to that which took place in 1935, and could well cancel out most of the preceding tax climate improvement efforts. Thus, Pennsylvania in a period of thirty-five years has traveled a complete circle with respect to its policy of reliance on direct corporation taxes to meet its general spending needs. It should be pointed out that the recent corporate tax increases were truly desperation measures and, being subject to reconsideration, may not represent a permanent shift of state tax policy.

Some Observations

This review of the changing picture of business tax policies in Pennsylvania and its parallel history of tax studies, most of which featured interstate business tax comparisons, is admittedly limited and thus clearly does not justify universally applicable conclusions. This course of events, however, justifies some observations which, though applicable to one state, may bear upon the approaches, methods, and usefulness of interstate industrial tax comparisons by other states, at least under similar circumstances.

I have not endeavored, nor do I believe it is part of my assignment, to join the argument as to the influence which tax policies and costs may or may not exert on industrial location and expansion decisions. Many persuasive reasons have been set forth to discount the importance of this factor among the many involved in industrial location decisions. Nevertheless, business tax burdens, being uniquely subject to public policy control, may have special significance as an indicator of official attitudes toward business and industry. In any event, recurring requests for information on Pennsylvania's relative tax climate coming from public and private industrial development agencies and from policy-making officials, would indicate that they feel the importance of such information justifies the time and effort required to produce it.

As to the methodology employed in interstate tax burden comparisons, Pennsylvania's experience in the use of virtually all known methods of comparison offers evidence to support some of their widely publicized shortcomings. Prominent among these have been the inadequacy and sometimes inaccuracies of tax and economic data; the lack of clear and standardized definitions of terms; the difficulties of classifying and identifying both the direct and indirect incidence of taxes on business; and the pitfalls involved in interpreting and comparing complex state and local tax laws and administrative practices.

An experience of the recent Governor's Tax Study and Revision Commission illustrates very well the pitfalls inherent in the lack of uniform terminology. In recommending that a balanced distribution of tax burdens between corporate and personal taxes be maintained, the committee referred to the then-current Pennsylvania ratio of approximately 30 percent business and 70 percent individual shares. Contrary to the committee's intent, this ratio was widely quoted and accepted as a magic formula for maintaining a favorable industrial tax climate. This led to a number of challenges as to its accuracy, with various groups claiming that the share allocated to business was considerably lower than the 30 percent level.

Clearly, this discrepancy resulted from the use of varying definitions of "business" taxes, applied against various definitions of state "income," which might include total revenues, or total tax revenues, or unrestricted tax revenues. One legislative leader, claiming that business was actually contributing only 25 percent rather than 30 percent of the state's income, suggested that business taxes be raised immediately to bring them up to the "magic" level of 30 percent. Clearly, in this instance, the use of a measurement factor subject to varying definitions of component terms resulted in confusing, rather than clarifying, the tax picture.

Despite the problems involved, Pennsylvania's history of tax studies and interstate comparisons evidences what I would hope is a general pattern of improvement and refinement of methodology. An example is the recent practice of utilizing and combining various methods of interstate comparison in a single presentation, thus exploiting the peculiar advantages of each method while compensating for its shortcomings.

As to the policy uses to which interstate tax burden comparisons are put, and their effectiveness, Pennsylvania's experience would indicate that these are dictated to a considerable extent by political and economic circumstances, and that the results of tax studies might often have a cumulative and delayed impact on public policy decisions. For example, the dozen studies made prior to 1955, the findings of which concurred in urging that Pennsylvania rely less heavily upon industry taxes, were undoubtedly instrumental in launching a conscious tax policy shift toward an improved business tax climate—but not until the economic timing was inspired by the postwar nationwide upsurge of industrial expansion, and not until the political timing was made feasible by prior adoption of an expandable and productive broad-based sales tax.

The studies made during the 1960s were instrumental in preserving the newly improved industrial tax climate and in influencing such refinements as a fiscal restructuring of the almost bankrupt unemployment compensation system. The acceptance and implementation of policy recommendations resulting from studies made during this period were made economically and politically feasible by the pro-industrial development attitudes of two successive politically influential governors, Governors Lawrence and Scranton, and by the relative absence of serious budget-balancing problems.

By contrast, recommendations of the most recent Governor's Tax Study and Revision Commission which called for maintaining the relatively favorable status of state industry tax burdens were ignored, at least temporarily, by the legislature. Faced with a preelection political impasse, it chose to risk endangering Pennsylvania's industrial attractiveness by sharply hiking business taxes, rather than to risk political recrimination by adopting a new personal income tax.

These experiences might indicate that, in terms of their influence on tax policy decisions, the results of comparative tax studies can be expected to support and encourage official action if and when such action is otherwise politically feasible. Whether or not their findings and recommendations have been ignored, or have been utilized immediately or ultimately, the numerous comparative tax studies undertaken in Pennsylvania played an important and desirable role in providing basic factual and analytical information to policy-making public officials, who share the unenviable responsibility of structuring a utopian state and local tax system which will meet all service demands, satisfy all political constituents, and at the same time will preserve and nourish economic growth and development.

From the standpoint of their use in industrial development promotional activities, it is quite obvious in Pennsylvania that the advertising effectiveness of interstate business tax comparisons is limited to periods when industry tax burdens are trending on the "down side" rather than the "up side."

Experience has also shown that comparative tax study results can have a backlash effect when exploited by industrial development groups in competing states. Findings that the state in question is in an unfavorable tax status, though perhaps useful in influencing corrective policy action in that state, can in the hands of competing states be used to convince industrial prospects that such a high-tax state should be avoided. On the other hand, studies which produce findings to show that the home state is in a favorable industrial tax position compared with other states can influence legislators to look to business taxes when they are next pressed for new sources of revenue.

I would conclude by venturing to predict that interstate business tax comparisons, despite their inherent faults, will continue to be in demand and will continue to be produced, at least in Pennsylvania, and probably in other states under similar circumstances. Let us hope that they also will be the objects of studious criticism, which will be sufficiently positive to encourage steady improvements in methodology and use, along with improvement of the availability of accurate and adequate information and the ready exchange of data on state and local taxing practices. A promising development is the appointment by the National Tax Association of a subcommittee on comparative tax burdens, charged with the function of investigating methods of interstate tax comparisons and developing uniformity in those methods.

I predict also that the subject of interstate tax comparisons will continue to occupy a prominent place on the agendas of future Tax Institute of America meetings. With that in mind, a single line quotation, which without attribution occupies an entire flyleaf of an early Pennsylvania tax study, offers an appropriate conclusion and a prediction: ". . . and that which we had hammered was again and again brought back to the anvil. . . ."

Appendix A

Reports of Pennsylvania Tax Studies
Published 1925 through 1969

Pennsylvania Tax Commission. *Report to the General Assembly, Commonwealth of Pennsylvania*. Harrisburg, 1925.
_____ . *Final Report*. Harrisburg, 1927.
Pennsylvania State Chamber of Commerce. *Report on Comparative Study of Corporate Taxes in Fifteen Industrial States*. By Clarence L. Turner. Harrisburg, 1938. 30 pp.
Pennsylvania Industrial Tax Survey Committee. *Report to the General Assembly*. Harrisburg, 1939.

Pennsylvania Industrial Tax Survey Committee. *Supplemental Report.* By Israel Stiefel. Harrisburg, 1939.

Pennsylvania Joint State Government Commission. *First Report on the Tax and Financial Problems of the Commonwealth of Pennsylvania to the General Assembly.* Harrisburg, 1941.

Pennsylvania Postwar Planning Commission. *Pennsylvania State Fiscal Policy and Taxation.* Harrisburg, 1943.

Pennsylvania Joint State Government Commission. Committee on Continuation of the Tax Study. *Tax Structure and Revenues of the General Fund of the Commonwealth of Pennsylvania 1913-1943.* Report No. 8. Harrisburg, 1944. 133 pp.

————. *Proposals for Revision of the Tax Structure of the Commonwealth of Pennsylvania.* A Report by the Tax Advisory Committee. Report No. 11. Harrisburg, 1945. 262 pp.

Pennsylvania Budget Bureau. *Relative Corporate Tax Burden in Pennsylvania and Eight Other Eastern States.* By Edw. B. Logan and Floyd Chalfant. Harrisburg, 1945.

Pennsylvania State Chamber of Commerce. *A Comparative Study of Business Taxes and Industrial Trends in Pennsylvania and Other States.* Bulletin No. 124. Harrisburg, 1948. 28 pp.

Pennsylvania Joint State Government Commission. Tax Study Committee. *Report of Findings and Recommendations on the Pennsylvania Tax System.* Harrisburg, 1949. Part I, 51 pp.; Part II, 16 pp.

Pennsylvania Emergency Tax and Revenue Fact Finding Committee. *Report: Let the Facts Speak for Themselves.* Harrisburg, 1951. 70 pp.

Pennsylvania State Tax Conference. Tax Reform Committee. *Report.* Harrisburg, 1952.

Pennsylvania Tax Study Committee. Alfred G. Buehler, Chairman. *The Tax Problem: Report.* Harrisburg, 1953. 329 pp.

————. *The Tax Problem: Second Report.* Harrisburg, 1955. 197 pp. *Conclusions*, 29 pp. *Appendix*, 50 pp.

Pennsylvania Economy League, Inc., Western Division. *The Relative Tax Cost to Manufacturing Industry: A Comparison of Pennsylvania with Several Other States.* Pittsburgh, 1956. 117 pp.

Pennsylvania Tax Policy Advisory Committee. *Report.* Harrisburg, 1956. 27 pp.

Pennsylvania Economy League, Inc., Western Division. *The Relative Tax Cost to Manufacturing Industry: 1956 Revision—A New Comparison of Pennsylvania with Several Other States.* Pittsburgh, 1957. 86 pp.

Pennsylvania Tax Advisory Committee. *Report.* Harrisburg, 1959.

Pennsylvania Department of Commerce. *Pennsylvania's Improved Tax Climate.* Harrisburg, 1960.

Pennsylvania Economy League. Eastern Division. *Comparative Tax, Water and Sewer Costs for Philadelphia and Eighty-one Other Municipalities in Pennsylvania, New Jersey, Delaware and Maryland.* Philadelphia, 1960.

Pennsylvania Economy League, Inc., State Division. *Taxes Paid by Industry: A Comparative Study of State-Local Tax Costs to Industry for General Government Purposes and for Unemployment Compensation in Pennsylvania and Ten Other States*. Harrisburg, 1962. 117 pp.

Pennsylvania Department of Commerce. *Pennsylvania's Improved Tax Climate*. Harrisburg, 1964.

Pennsylvania Economy League, Inc., State Division. *Taxes Paid by Industry*. Harrisburg, 1967.

Pennsylvania Governor's Tax Study and Revision Commission. *Interim Report*. Harrisburg, 1967.

———. *Final Long Range Report*. Harrisburg, 1968. 93 pp.

Pennsylvania Economy League, Inc., State Division. *A Supplement to Taxes Paid by Industry: An Updating of and Supplement to the Report of December, 1967*. Harrisburg, 1969. 32 pp.

**A New Development in
the Measurement of Business
and Nonbusiness State
and Local Tax Burdens**

Allen D. Manvel

A new development in the measurement of business and nonbusiness state and local tax burdens is found in the forthcoming study of "Measuring the Fiscal Capacity and Effort of State and Local Areas"[1] which the Advisory Commission on Intergovernmental Relations has been conducting during the past 18 months.

Some of you may recall a Commission study of similar title issued in 1962.[2] That report provided state-by-state comparisons of estimated tax capacity, together with related measures of "relative tax effort." The present study goes considerably further, in several ways: to deal with nontax revenue sources as well as taxes; to develop comparisons for metropolitan areas and several hundred counties as well as for entire states; and to provide comparative measures separately for state and local government revenue sources, as well as on a composite basis.

Measuring Revenue Capacity

In this study, the method used to estimate revenue capacity resembles earlier efforts to measure the relative financing ability of various states under a so-called model tax system. With that approach, each state's capacity was calculated by determining the potential yield obtainable from a predetermined uniform model set of taxes and tax rates. But there is no consensus about what an ideal state and local revenue system should be. So, instead of postulating some hypothetical or model pattern, existing practices are taken as a starting point in the Commission study. In other words, *revenue capacity* for any particular area is defined as *the amount of money that would be raised if the governments serving the area were making use, at national average rates, of each of the numerous kinds of revenue sources employed by state and local governments*. With this approach, the weight given to each particular component is determined by its relative importance in the nationwide state-local revenue system. For example, using 1967 as the reference year, nontax sources altogether account for 21 percent of the total weighting, property taxes for 32 percent, sales and gross receipts taxes for 27 percent, and so forth.

But the subclassification of revenue applied was far more detailed than this illustration might suggest, involving some twenty-three type-of-tax categories and an even larger number of nontax components. For each detailed source, the potential yield at the national average rate was estimated for individual states and local areas, and the resulting figures were added to obtain an estimate of revenue capacity for each area.

In the earlier Commission study, this procedure was described as involving a "representative tax system" approach, while in the present study—in view of the broader coverage—the term "average financing system" is applied. A similar set of calculations has been used in Canada since 1967 as the basis for allocating annual revenue equalization grants to each of the provincial governments found to have less revenue capacity per capita than the national average. The Canadian estimates take account of sixteen categories of provincial revenue.

One of the most challenging aspects of the Commission study concerned appropriate ways to measure the potential yield of various nontax revenue sources. However, I shall not discuss that matter now, in view of our main present concern with tax comparisons, except to note that some areas show up quite differently in relative capacity and effort when all revenue sources are taken into account, rather than only taxes. This may not be surprising, but the explicit quantification of the differences should be one illuminating feature of the report.

Treatment of Property Tax

In the earlier Commission study, the property tax was treated as a single revenue source. In other words, although the estimate of each state's property tax base was built up in terms of various components, a single nationwide average rate was then applied to the aggregate base figure for each state, to estimate its property tax capacity. For the present study, in contrast, potential-yield estimates were developed separately for five property tax components, i.e., state property taxes and local property taxes upon nonfarm residential realty, farm property, vacant lots, and business property.

Since no distribution of actual collections by type of property is available, it was necessary at the outset to estimate the yield of local property taxes in each state for the several classes I have mentioned. That was done by reference to assessed value figures reported in the 1967 Census of Governments. It was also possible from that Census and from Agriculture Department data to estimate the market value of taxable residential, farm, and vacant lot property in various states, metropolitan areas, and major counties. In the main, this involved expanding assessed values to full-value amounts by reference to sales ratios developed for taxable realty in the 1967 Census of Governments. But sales ratio data for commercial and industrial real estate are limited and spotty at best, and a considerable part of the property taxation of business relates to personal property rather than real estate. Hence, it was necessary to estimate *indirectly* the potential yield of the local property tax as applied in its "representative" form to business property in various states and local areas.

For this purpose, a set of proxy measures was applied to each of fifty-six types of nonfarm business. The procedure involved five major steps:

1. Working separately with nationwide amounts for land, inventories, and other forms of business property holdings, to develop a set of nationwide market-value estimates by type of business.
2. Using these figures to estimate the amount of all local property tax revenue that, on a uniform-rate basis, would be attributable to each business class.
3. Calculating the indicated amount of property tax per dollar of earnings originating in each business class. (As calculated in the national income and product accounts, "earnings" consists of payrolls and other labor income plus proprietors' business income.)
4. Applying these national average ratios to the amount of earnings estimated by the Office of Business Economics for each of the types of business in various state and local areas.
5. Aggregating these detailed figures for each area to arrive at an estimate of the area's local business property tax capacity.

In the nation as a whole, this component made up about one-eighth of the revenue capacity of state and local governments, or about one-sixth of their total tax capacity. But when considered in relation to the own-source revenue of local governments alone, the share of business property taxation was about twice as great, i.e., about one-fourth of their total revenue capacity or one-third of their tax capacity, as estimated by reference to revenue arrangements prevailing in 1967.

Business Property Tax Share

As would be expected, there is considerable variation from state to state, and even more among individual counties, in the proportion of all revenue capacity that is represented by the business property tax component. The Commission study reports this proportion, as well as that for other revenue sources, for individual states, metropolitan areas, and several hundred counties. It also supplies comparative data on relative effort for various sources, expressing the percentage relationship between estimated capacity and actual receipts. Relative effort is so measured specifically for local business property taxes on a state-by-state basis (but not for particular local areas), and great interstate diversity is shown. An effort index for local property taxation of business amounting to less than half the national average appears for five states (Alabama, Alaska, Delaware, Kentucky, and Pennsylvania), while at the other extreme this index is at least 50 percent above the national average in the four states of California, Idaho, Montana, and South Dakota.

As the Commission report emphasizes, comparisons of this kind reflect inter-state differences not only in the prevailing effective *rate* of local property taxes but also in the scope of such taxes as applied to business. For example, although business inventories and movable equipment are taxable in most states, this is not so in such states as Delaware, Hawaii, New York, and Pennsylvania. Again, while public utilities are predominately subject to local property taxation, some states have provided for their exemption from the local tax base in favor of some other form of exaction. For the states involved, such departures from the "representative" version of the local property tax that was postulated in estimating potential yields will make the effort index for business property taxes lower than it would otherwise be.

Business and Personal Taxes Distinguished

This problem is overcome to some degree in another part of the Commission report, where certain revenue components are grouped to show capacity and effort measures for business taxes and personal taxes respectively.

As most narrowly defined for this purpose, business taxes consist of corporation income, severance, and local property taxes on business. Together, these sources make up 18 percent of all state-local revenue capacity nationwide, but this proportion ranges from less than 10 percent in some rural states up to more than 25 percent in Louisiana. When the business tax concept is broadened to include also local taxes on farm property, the nationwide proportion of all revenue capacity is raised to nearly 21 percent, with individual state percentages running from 15 to 31 percent.

In the report, personal taxes are also defined in alternative ways—narrowly, to comprise individual income taxes, all general and selective sales taxes, and death taxes; and more broadly to include also local taxes on nonfarm residential property. The narrower definition involves 36 percent of all state-local revenue capacity nationwide, while the broader grouping accounts for 51 percent of the aggregate. Excluded from both the business and personal tax groupings are a number of other taxes, as well as nontax sources, together making up 30 percent of all own-source revenue of state and local governments.

These concepts of business taxes and personal taxes are obviously arbitrary. If the comparison of business tax loads had been a primary objective, rather than only an incidental phase of the Commission study, a somewhat more sophisticated approach might well have been considered. For example, one might try to allocate to business some estimated share of various kinds of sales taxes and of motor vehicle taxes. It should be noted, however, that any such adjustments would need to apply to both the capacity and actual-revenue sides of the ledger, so that for many states, at least, the resulting other measure of relative business tax effort would probably resemble that indicated by the simpler grouping which was actually employed.

Interstate Tax Comparisons of Business Tax Burdens

In any event, I believe you may be interested in some highlights of these interstate comparisons of business tax loads. For simplicity, these observations will involve only the narrower concept, excluding farm property taxes. It should be remembered, of course, that the data being considered are for fiscal 1967.

As of that year, business tax capacity was being tapped at least 25 percent more heavily than the national average in a half-dozen states—California, Idaho, Massachusetts, Michigan, Minnesota, and New York. At the other extreme were seven states where the effort index for business taxation, as defined in the report, was at least 30 percent below the national average: Alabama, Illinois, Kentucky, Missouri, Nebraska, Washington, and West Virginia. Each group obviously includes states that are economically and demographically diverse, as well as geographically scattered. It would appear, then, that the relative intensity of business taxation depends a good deal upon historical traditions and the political balance of power in various areas, rather than resulting directly from particular social or economic conditions.

Perhaps something can be learned also by looking at the intensity of business taxation in relation to the overall level of state-local revenue effort. For this purpose, we might consider two groups of states—the thirteen with an overall effort index at least 5 points above the national average in 1967, and the thirteen at the other extreme, where revenue effort was at least 9 points below the national average. In the high-effort group, only two states (Alaska and Hawaii) had a below-average level of business taxation. In six of the thirteen the effort index for business taxes was at least 10 points higher than the particular state's overall index of revenue effort; in one it was 9 points higher, in four practically the same, and in only two (those previously mentioned) was it materially lower.

A quite different picture appears for the thirteen lowest-effort states. Only one of them (Louisiana) showed an effort index for business taxes above the national average. In only two cases was the business effort index at least 10 points above the state's overall index of revenue effort (even though that index, it will be recalled, was well below the nationwide norm), and in four of these states the business effort index was at least 10 points below the composite revenue-effort measure.

It would thus appear that the relative intensity of business taxation is closely tied up with overall fiscal responsiveness. Where a particular state (together with its local governments) is tapping its revenue capacity at a greater than average

Table 8-1
Selected Measures of State-Local Revenue Capacity and Effort for the Ten Most Populous States: 1967

	Calif.	Fla.	Ill.	Mass.	Mich.	N.J.	N.Y.	Ohio	Penna.	Texas
Revenue capacity per capita:										
Amount	$496	$407	$432	$385	$415	$412	$447	$384	$342	$381
Index (U.S. average = 100)	125	103	109	97	105	104	113	97	86	96
Actual revenue per capita:										
Amount	$521	$376	$366	$432	$419	$387	$562	$333	$339	$318
Index (U.S. average = 100)	131	95	92	109	106	98	142	84	85	80
Relative revenue effort (actual revenue/revenue capacity, in percent):										
All state-local sources	105	92	85	112	101	94	126	87	99	84
All taxes	108	84	84	121	100	97	138	82	99	75
Property taxes	122	79	94	141	103	137	125	94	82	89
Local taxes on business property	151	89	82	114	104	91	125	107	47	94
"Business" taxes:										
Excl. farm property taxes[1]	141	86	62	129	94	85	135	88	78	90
Incl. farm property taxes	140	87	71	130	96	86	136	90	80	84
"Personal" taxes:										
Total	98	80	86	115	95	102	145	77	107	67
Residential nonfarm property taxes	106	72	101	166	97	176	127	85	121	89
Other "personal" taxes[2]	94	85	80	93	94	68	155	73	101	61

Source: Advisory Commission on Intergovernmental Relations, *Measuring the Fiscal Capacity and Effort of State and Local Areas*, Report M-58, Washington: Government Printing Office, 1971, Appendix G.

[1] Corporation income, severance, and local property taxes on business.

[2] Personal income, general and selective sales, and death taxes.

rate, it is likely to be relying even more heavily upon business taxation. On the other hand, the limited use of business taxation is generally associated with below-average levels of financing effort for other sources also.

In Table 8-1 (above) there is a set of illustrative figures from the Commission report, with regard to the ten most populous states. I hope they may increase the interest in seeing this publication.

But it should be emphasized especially that this study was not undertaken merely or primarily to provide such comparative data for their own sake. Rather, it was a research effort to explore the problems involved in developing meaningful measures of the relative fiscal capacity and effort of various areas. Accordingly, the report includes a detailed description of the concepts, methods, and sources employed to develop the figures presented; a discussion of the prospect for recurrent and better measures of this kind; and chapters considering some of the ways that such data may be useful for policy making and fiscal administration at various levels of government.

I very much hope that many of you will wish to go beyond an examination of the report's illustrative statistical findings, to consider carefully and critically the balance of the study, and its methodological sections in particular.

Notes

1. Advisory Commission on Intergovernmental Relations, *Measuring the Fiscal Capacity and Effort of State and Local Areas*, Report M-58 (Washington, D.C.: Government Printing Office, 1971), 209 pp.

2. Advisory Commission on Intergovernmental Relations, *Measures of State and Local Fiscal Capacity and Tax Effort*, Report M-16 (Washington, D.C., 1962), 150 pp.

Discussion of Policy Implications of Quantitative Distribution of Tax Burden

Chairman Arthur P. Becker, *University of Wisconsin–Milwaukee:* I am going to take the liberty of asking the first question. It will be addressed to Professor Due.

I was very much interested in your notion that all taxes essentially are business taxes, and that the distinction between nonbusiness and business taxes is not as great as many people believe it to be. Now if this is so, then why do you advocate nonbusiness taxes?

Professor John F. Due, *University of Illinois:* I don't know that I was advocating nonbusiness taxes if you accept my idea that all taxes can be regarded as either business taxes or nonbusiness taxes! What I was saying was: I think there is some objection to heavy levies of the type traditionally labeled business taxes. This is quite another matter from the point raised in your question.

One of the great troubles with some of these so-called business taxes is that we have no notion of what the distributional pattern is. How is the burden of a capital stock tax distributed? How is the burden of the portion of the sales tax on producers' goods distributed? There are two completely different schools of thought on this. One is that these taxes end up in the prices of the final products, and therefore, in a very haphazard way are relative to consumption expenditures. Another is that they have the effect of reducing the return on savings. One thing is sure, and that is that we don't know.

We don't even know too well the distributional effect of the property tax, particularly the portion falling on business firms. You can't talk about the equity of a tax unless you know who really bears the burden of the reduction of real income as a result. Since this is also obscure, it seems to me there is some good reason for minimizing the reliance on these taxes. This is not so true of the corporate income tax which is essential as a part of the overall income tax structure. But some of these other levies are objectionable if for no other reason than their unknown distributional patterns plus, of course, the adverse effects they may have on business firms, locational decision making, and many other things.

Chairman Becker: I take it then from your answer that, to be on the safe side, we need taxes of both kinds.

Dr. John Shannon, *Advisory Commission on Intergovernmental Relations:* I would like to make three quick comments on some rather harsh observations that Professor Due had to make on some estimates that we had prepared on this subject.

The first is a recognition of the wisdom of his criticism about our solution of the initial payments made by business in the sales tax field. Professor Stocker made the same observation this morning. Lloyd Slater and several others have also pointed out this omission. So in our revised compilation we do build in an estimate on the sales tax front, albeit not a perfect one. We assume that 20 percent of all sales taxes are initially paid by business firms. Now obviously there are going to be variations among the states, but at least we have tried to acknowledge that very legitimate criticism and plug it up as best we can. There are other shortcomings. We haven't been able to estimate the amount of motor vehicles receipts initially paid by business firms.

The second criticism, however, I think represents a vast overstatement of our own position. We have never used the term in our tables "taxes on business." We have carefully inserted on every one of our tables the term "the relationship of state and local taxes with an initial impact on business to total state and local taxes." This is to tip off legislators and others that there is a difference between initial impact and final incidence, and in the report from which this table was developed, we hammered home at the capriciousness—as Professor Due has pointed out—with respect to the final incidence of business taxation. This is also one of the basic reasons why we on the Commission tend to concur with the idea of placing as much emphasis as possible on personal taxes and to play down those taxes that have an initial impact on business because we cannot clearly calculate the ricochet effects.

The third observation—John, you are still on the ACIR mailing list.

Professor Don M. Soule, *University of Kentucky:* If we followed the policy of moving away from so-called business taxes toward only personal taxes, does the panel feel that the tax effort would generally stay the same, go up, or go down?

Chairman Becker: Allen, since you addressed yourself primarily to the tax effort, would you like to start this off?

Mr. Allen D. Manvel, *Advisory Commission on Intergovernmental Relations:* Two parts to the answer. I suppose the question could be interpreted as saying if the tax structure were making more use of personal taxes, would people favor spending more or less. And I suppose that, unless all the politicians are wrong, a shift in that direction might have a dampening effect on levels of public expenditure rather than otherwise.

On the other hand, there is a more technical way that this could be interpreted, and it runs like this: Supposing the revenue system were different, what difference would it make in the relative financing capability of different areas? We did explore that matter somewhat in the Commission study, hypothesizing, for example, that in 1967 income and death taxes together had been yielding three times as much as they were at the state and local government levels, with an offsetting reduction in certain other combinations of other taxes, to see what this did to patterns of capacity.

We were somewhat surprised that that much of a substitution made as little difference as it did in relative capacity at the state level.

Chairman Becker: John, would you like to answer this question, too.

Professor Due: I would like to come back just a moment to the comments from Mr. Shannon. You see, what I am really concerned about is the labels that are applied and the consequences of the use of the percentages based on these labels. I know that you say in your heading "Taxes With Initial Impact on Business." But then I can't see how you exclude the retail sales tax because clearly its impact is on business. But the main point I want to make is this: You establish figures of certain percentages from personal taxes and percentages from taxes with initial impact on business, or taxes on business, or business taxes, or whatever you label them, and then these are picked up by people promoting particular tax policies, or people looking for additional revenue in the states. Here is a state that is getting only 20 percent of its revenue from taxes with an initial impact on business, and the national average, say, is 30 percent. Thus persons advocate getting additional revenue from business taxes. But it may be that the particular so-called business taxes that the state is using are ones that have a particularly bad effect on the economy of the state. The fact that they are only yielding 20 percent of the total is really not the relevant consideration because of the very harmful effects they have. In other words, to me these percentages are misleading; they lead to misleading interpretations and may well lead to the wrong direction in policy. Once the percentages are printed, they are taken as gospel fact—that this is how much business is paying in the state.

Chairman Becker: Thank you.

Dr. Lloyd E. Slater, *New York State Deputy Commissioner for Tax Research:* I have a question for Mr. Manvel. I have not previously seen the figures and studied your report as presented, but I am bothered. You show New York State as making a tremendous tax effort which I am sure is greatly overstated. I feel in all modesty that somehow we have to get to the bottom of where the errors are, as I feel there definitely are errors. Now my main reason for feeling that certain of these figures are overstated is that rather recently I had the occasion to make a very rough measure of the tax effort in New York in which I related our total state and local taxes to personal income and compared our percentage of personal income to the national average.

I started back in about 1929, and I didn't use every year in between. I used a number, and I don't have the table with me, but in the early period both New York State and the national average had state and local taxes that represented roughly 7 percent of our personal income. We have gotten up now to where the national average is about 14 percent. In New York it is about 11 percent. As much as we have increased taxes, we haven't increased them in New York as greatly in relation to personal income as the rest of the country. Yet you come up with figures that show us making a great effort. I am just trying to think why this could be.

We don't tax personal property, for example. I don't know what adjustment you may have made. We have that capacity, but we aren't utilizing it, and the tax rates we have on property are higher on the property that we do tax, but we don't tax so much of it. If all you did was take assessed values and expand them to full values on your equalization rates, you perhaps didn't get our full potential, at least for personal property.

I also suspect that New York has a greater percentage of tax-exempt property than most of the states. We have the United Nations. We have a lot of federal and state facilities, and we have a lot of religious properties. Because the values of those properties are never accurate enough to use in research work, I suspect—without being able to prove it—that we have a bigger potential in relation to property which we have chosen for one reason or another to exempt than many other states do.

Now, we have a potential to collect a tax on stock transfer that I think would be unavailable in any other state, and we are utilizing that potential. No other state that has a stock exchange is trying to do so. Their exchanges are not sufficiently developed to the point that they would feel they could afford to do that. Only two or three states do have the stock transfer tax other than New York, and none of them have an exchange. It is possible that this revenue inflates our tax effort. It is an effort that is peculiar to New York.

I would like to meet with you and talk with you, but I wonder in my question if you have any observation as to how you could reconcile the results from your study and the fact that as a percentage of personal income, New York has not been quite keeping up with the national average.

Mr. Manvel: There is a question on your last comment of whether you are talking about historical trends or an actual relationship. If one takes the more traditional historical kind of interstate comparison that has been used in census reports and otherwise for a long time—namely, state and local tax revenue relative to resident personal income of the state—it has surely been my impression that New York has shown up well above the national average on that score, up near the top of the list.

Dr. Slater: No, no.

Mr. Manvel: In general, the measures we get show the older eastern and north central industrial states as having somewhat less revenue capacity relative to the national average. I am not saying that they are below the national average. I am saying their standing is less in our kind of measure than it is in resident personal income terms. We took Pennsylvania as an example to try to explore some of the factors, and in that state there are two.

First, there is the fact that these older northeastern and north central residential states with lots of fairly old cities in them include a considerable portion of multifamily, older residential housing stock, and given the kind of approach to the measurement of capacity that we are employing here, where residential, urban property values make up, I can't remember the exact percentage, about 15 or 16 percent of the total, this results in such states having less value per capita relative to income per capita than it does in other kinds of states. Now that is one factor.

Second, as you get the most mature kind of economic activity—the type of thing that is illustrated by New York City, and even more by some of the big, central cities in the northeast, where the shift relatively in terms of economic activity is away from manufacturing within the central city and increasingly towards services, including governmental centers and the like—then the amount of capacity relative to income of the area that is represented by the business property tax base is declining secularly. There is less taxable property per X dollars of earnings, as you move from manufacturing toward distribution toward service.

We know this generally, and I think this is another factor in these older, more mature service-oriented areas. The ultimate of this, of course, is where you get a center that is heavily governmental, as you indicate. In that case, as to business property capacity, those earnings that come out of public employees in those areas, nothing is credited for business property tax capacity in this construct.

So these are some of the implications, but I would never claim that we may not have made some errors, or that our estimating bases are the best that one can conceive. They are not, I am sure.

I don't think that we are starting from a common base in our discussion because it is my impression that on the traditional terms also New York State would show up as one of the highest tax effort states in recent years.

Dr. Slater: I didn't make it clear, I am sure, but I meant to ask specifically what adjustment you have made for our present exemption of personal property and the fact that we had an ability there that wasn't recognized on our tax roll.

Mr. Manvel: The exemptions are not built in as such at all. The potential tax base is calculated on the assumption of no exemptions of privately owned residential property, for example, vacant lots, business property and so on.

Dr. Slater: I mean as compared with other states that tax personal property, inventories, machinery and equipment, even though the personal property tax has been declining, what adjustment have you made for the fact that we have a capacity there that we have chosen not to shcw on our tax rolls?

Mr. Manvel: I made a brief reference to that. In estimating the potential capacity from any revenue source, one has to assume a common definition of that kind of source. Think of the sales tax we had to work with—the "general" sales tax. We had to look at the practices of the country. This was done in the earlier Commission study, too. Decide, was it a general sales tax? Did it extend to sales of food? Did it extend to this, that, or the other? And then determine from that what form we were assuming for the sales tax.

Carrying it over to the property tax side, we have said that the representative version of local general property taxes includes utilities. It includes all private residential property. It includes all farm property, all business property, and includes with business property not only land and structures, but movable equipment and inventories.

Now we know that isn't 100 percent true everywhere in the country. In fact, in New York as you say, there are very strong exceptions. That says that that piece of capacity we have included for New York State as to business credits New York with business property tax capacity that assumes a version of the tax that is broader than you have, and to the extent that we have estimates of yield from business property, that relationship will come in lower than it would if your coverage were representative.

Dr. Slater: I think this probably fully explains the difference that I am concerned about. I think it would bring the figure down if we added it in, and it would also account for the fact that we have gotten as much as $300 million a year from the stock transfer tax, and a few peculiar things of that sort: Special rating.

Mr. Arthur L. Cunkle, *Florida Legislative Service Bureau:* I would like to tell a brief story that would illustrate a number of the points that have been made here today. For a number of years—long before the days of ACIR and its recommendations—we have been trying to reduce the tax on business inventories. We were passing these statutes, but our courts would throw them out as unconstitutional.

In 1965 we proposed, and the following year the people approved, a constitutional amendment authorizing a fractional assessment of inventories, and so in 1967 we came to implement it. These data are obviously not in Mr. Manvel's study. We didn't know what inventories there were in the state. There was about $6 billion worth of personal property recorded, but nobody knew what part of this was inventory. Our sample studies that the few assessors made indicated at least 75 percent. That means the local governments were getting at least $100 million from the business inventories tax, and so in 1967 we proposed that it would be reduced by half in 1968 and to one-fourth in 1969.

When our personal property assessments came in in 1968, after cutting this roll in half, the figures county by county in each of 67 counties were almost identical with what they had been the year before, and the state officials didn't know whether this was before the 50 percent exemption or after. But as they collected the taxes on it, it must have been afterwards. In 1969 when we cut it in half again, the figures were still identical.

We wondered if we could cut it in half each successive year without any loss of revenue. Apparently about the only explanation anyone could give for this interesting little experience is that the assessors just went out and found enough additional property to replace that which was exempt. There is one other point that might make it interesting. We originally wrote this as exempting stock in trade. So the stock was interpreted by the courts to mean cows and horses, and then they went on to say that Mr. Busch was a tradesman, and therefore, his multi-million dollar brewery was stock in trade.

Mr. Gerald D. Hall, *New Jersey State Chamber of Commerce:* I would like to issue something of a challenge to any one of the panelists. I can only regard as somewhat half cooked any studies of business tax burden or comparisons between jurisdictions that exclude the statutory benefit taxes, i.e., unemployment compensation and disability benefit taxes. Workmen's compensation, of course, is quite different as between the states, but it is also a very substantial cost factor. My experience with the several thousand members of the New Jersey State Chamber of Commerce has been that they get more excited over increases in unemployment taxes, for instance, than they do over proposed corporation tax increases, sales tax increases, or whatever. These are very real matters as John well knows. Illinois, for instance, enjoys a preferable position in workmen's compensation costs as compared to New Jersey and New York. It is a very real factor in business attraction and retention. I believe such costs must be included in any valid comparison of statutory cost burdens.

Mr. John W. Ingram, *Pennsylvania Economy League, Inc.:* Jerry, I think you are right. I think to omit utility charges, particularly those of publicly owned utilities, also leaves a big gap. The difficulty is trying somehow to measure them, particularly when you are using a hypothetical corporate model, because you have to construct such a complicated model with so many assumptions because of the complications in unemployment compensation systems that you are vulnerable to subjectivity and associated problems.

What we did instead in our studies was to compare, feature by feature, the major benefit provisions and the major financing provisions of the unemployment compensation systems of several industrial states. This, I think, produces some basis for at least qualified conclusions as to the weight of those taxes. However, the weight of unemployment compensation taxes in any year of itself is not very meaningful because, as in any insurance type fund, the annual contribution to a fund doesn't reflect necessarily the rate or ultimate burden of the benefit payments. A state may have a very low rate of taxation but may have a bankrupt fund or one that might be quickly bankrupt under conditions of severe unemployment, and this obviously would be a misleading comparison.

I think you are right about the need for comparing employee benefit contributions in such studies. I wish somebody would come up with a method that is useful, dependable, realistic and practicable to bring that about.

Professor Morris Beck, *Rutgers University:* May I come to the defense of the ACIR for a moment and at the same time try to resolve Dr. Slater's dilemma.

Until the ACIR published this 1962 data on tax capacity, there was no alternative to measuring tax burdens or tax effort except in relationship to personal income. New York being a very high income state—and I believe that the excess above the national average would be well above the 13 percent shown in Mr. Manvel's table—it is not surprising that you get a much lower effort by using personal income. But the benefit of the new study or the new data that Allen Manvel is preparing is that we now have a second means of measuring tax effort in the states by comparing the taxable revenue to some national reference point, and for individual states it will be necessary to make adjustments, but at least we now have a second benchmark against which to measure an effort of individual states.

Chairman Becker: We can have one last question.

Professor Soule: There is a tendency in many states, when they view findings like those for example, in Kentucky—which is very low in property taxes—to say, "We are way down toward the bottom." Then by simple computation you can say if we went up to the national level effort, we could get this many dollars, and you do that for all the taxes you are below average on, and add up the total. One of the adjustments which isn't always done is to say: "Let's take the one where we are above average, and let's subtract that out." I wonder if there has been any thought on that?

Mr. Manvel: Yes.

Chairman Becker: On that positive note, I can bring the afternoon session to a conclusion. Thank you for staying as long as you have.

Part III:
Local Taxation of Business

10 Thrust of New Developments in Local Taxation as It Affects Business

George F. Break

With the costs of existing local governmental services, demands for new urban programs, and public resistance to higher property tax rates all rising rapidly, many local governments in this country find themselves in an almost continuous state of fiscal crisis. This is especially true in the large metropolitan areas where lack of time and resources frequently means that new revenues are obtained from the most available sources rather than from those whose use would be most equitable and efficient from an economic point of view. In such an environment, business, with its high visibility to the ordinary citizen as a potential source of new tax revenues, has much to lose from inaction and much to gain from concerted efforts to assist in the eternal search for new and better systems of local taxation.

This paper takes for granted that the answer is not to be found solely in the reform of the property tax itself. Partly this reflects a judgment that the property tax suffers from major defects that are ineradicable, so that public resistance to increasing tax rates is not likely to abate. Partly it is based on a forecast that the expansion of the property tax base will not keep pace over the next decade with the demand for local government services, so that urban governments will more and more have to seek their additional revenues from nonproperty tax sources.

It is to the success of that search that business groups can make a major contribution. This will not, of course, be easy. Attitudes will have to be shifted, for one thing, from conditioned reflex opposition to all tax increases and fervent hopes for greatly increased efficiency in governmental operations to acceptance of the inevitability, and desirability, of higher tax rates. Given such a shift, attention can then be focused on the best means of raising the required revenues. This paper discusses a number of alternative sources which I believe are worth your serious consideration as the fiscal pressures in your own communities intensify.

Local Income Taxes

Three basic types of personal income tax, each with its own strengths and weaknesses, make attractive candidates for inclusion in any program of local tax reform.

95

A Proportional Surcharge

The first type of personal income tax is a proportional surcharge on state personal income tax liabilities. Exceedingly simple to administer, this plan would reproduce at the local level all of the features of the state personal income tax. It would, for example, make the local levy progressive in relation to total family income, and this constitutes one of its more controversial characteristics. To those who lament the failure of state and federal income taxes to do more than they presently do to moderate inequalities in the distribution of income, such a local tax, though its accomplishments in this respect would be modest at best, would still be a welcome addition to the fiscal system. Others, however, argue that redistributional taxation should be confined to the federal and state governments, or even to the federal government alone.

Partly this is a matter of principle, since the social benefits from a more equitable distribution of after-tax income in any specific jurisdiction are spread widely over the country as a whole, and partly it is a pragmatic necessity, since no local government can go much farther than its neighbors in the direction of a more equal distribution of income without risking such a loss of capital that its purpose becomes completely frustrated. All things considered, progressivity in a local income tax does not appear to be an essential requirement.

A Proportional Tax on Adjusted
Gross Income

The second type of personal income tax is a proportional tax on adjusted gross income reported on state personal income tax returns. Equally easy to administer, this tax would be based on the most comprehensive measure of individual abilities to pay that is reported on personal income tax returns, and would be capable of producing large amounts of revenue at relatively low tax rates.

It would, of course, have a strictly proportional rate structure for all taxpayers, and it would give rise to the familiar "notch" problem in the vicinity of the minimum-income filing requirement. That problem, however, would not be a serious one as long as the filing requirement was set at a low income level and the tax rate was held to modest dimensions. With a tax rate of 1 percent and a filing requirement of $600 a year, for example, a person increasing his income from $599 to $600 would, it is true, increase his local income tax liability from zero to $6, but this very high marginal tax rate would fall off rapidly as income rose above $600. Another problem with the use of adjusted gross income is that it is not, by general professional agreement, an ideal measure of ability to pay taxes, but it is available, and the gain in simplicity from using it may well be worth the accompanying loss in equity.

A Proportional Tax on Adjusted
Net Income

The third type of personal income tax is a proportional tax on adjusted *net* income computed from data given on state personal income tax returns. If gains in equity are judged to be worth some increase in complexity in a local income tax, its base may be derived from adjusted gross income by the subtraction of a limited number of personal deductions and exemptions. The most important appear to be some allowance for extraordinary medical expenses and large casualty losses, deductions for employee costs of earning income, including child care and education costs, and a general exemption of poverty-line budget costs for different-sized families.

With adjustments held to these minimum amounts, considerable revenue could be raised at low tax rates; alternatively, all of the personal deductions and exemptions allowed on state tax returns could be recognized simply by applying the local tax rate to the state personal income tax base. Calculations for California for 1965 show that the following tax rates would have provided equal amounts of revenue when applied to the four different tax bases just discussed:

Local Tax Base	Equi-yield Tax Rates
State personal income tax liabilities	50%
Adjusted gross income reported on state personal income tax returns	Less than 1/2%
Adjusted gross income minus a $3,000 personal exemption on each tax return	2/3%
Taxable income reported on state returns	1%

Psychological Barriers

Early enactment of one of these alternative local income tax plans, it is true, may be frustrated by the presence of either of two psychological barriers. It may be, for one thing, that in any given urban area a community that had the only local income tax would have a higher negative visibility, other things equal, than would the community with the highest property tax rate. While I am not convinced that this proposition is, or need be, true, it is clearly very much in the minds of local officials, who frequently resist the enactment of local income taxes unless the tax rate is to be uniform throughout the metropolitan area. The costs of such a policy are not only the delays inherent in the requirement of areawide agreement on local tax policies, but also the surrender of local fiscal autonomy through the inability of any one community to raise or lower its income tax rate in line with changes in its own fiscal needs.

The second psychological barrier is provided by the fears of many voters that enactment of any new local tax would lead to a faster growth of expenditures than would otherwise take place. This barrier to fiscal innovation has persisted because the proposition in question is an exceedingly difficult one to test empirically. Perhaps there is some truth to it, but it is certainly far from firmly established in the minds of most fiscal experts. The crucial question for local voters to ask themselves, therefore, is how much tax inequity and inefficiency they are willing to continue to accept in order to achieve a highly uncertain degree of expenditure retardation.

Difficulties Involved in Substitution for Property Levies

While neither of these barriers appears to be insurmountable, difficult problems of a different sort may arise if a local income tax is to be substituted for existing property levies rather than being used to finance future increases in local expenditures. A recent case study of San Francisco, by R. Stafford Smith, provides a useful illustration.[1] Assuming that the enactment of a local income tax would be accompanied by a proportionate reduction in property tax rates sufficient to maintain city tax revenues constant, Smith compares the effects of using ten alternative local income tax plans in this way on three broad groups of people— resident homeowners, resident renters, and owners of businesses located in the city.

Let me cite here a few of his findings for a 1 percent tax on total personal, corporate, and noncorporate business income in San Francisco, including incomes earned in that jurisdiction by nonresidents, computed from data for 1967.

Effect on Homeowners. For homeowners the net effect of substituting such a tax for an equal amount of existing property taxes would have been progressive in relation to family income, though the amounts of money involved would have been relatively small. Whereas families with an average annual income of only $2,000 a year would have enjoyed a net tax reduction of $60 in 1967, homeowners with an income of $10,000 would have about broken even, and those with an average income of $35,000 (the highest income group studied) would have paid nearly $90 more under the income tax than under the property tax. These estimates, of course, are based on average homeownership figures for each of the income groups distinguished, and considerable variation would no doubt exist around the average in each group.

Effect on Resident Renters. The most difficult group to analyze is resident renters. We can be reasonably certain that in the short run they would be worse off because they would be subject to the new local income tax but would enjoy no benefits, in the form of reduced rental payments, from the property tax reductions enacted on their dwelling units. In due course of time, however, housing rentals should become lower in income-tax cities than in municipalities that finance similar public services from property taxation. This would happen most quickly if the income-tax city were one part of a large urban area, because then the decline in demand for rental units in that city on the part of mobile tenants who could avoid the local income tax by living elsewhere would soon drive rental prices down.

Even if the new income tax were areawide, the higher rate of return from the ownership of rental housing brought about by the reduction in property taxes would stimulate building of such units, and over the course of a year or two, this additional building would make for lower rental prices than otherwise would have prevailed. The problem is, however, that these predicted renter benefits from a reduction in property taxes are uncertain both as to their amount and as to the speed with which they would occur.

Resident renters, therefore, are likely to take a highly skeptical view of any local tax reform plan that proposes to substitute an income tax for some part of existing property taxes. Smith's calculations for San Francisco in 1967, which were based on the more or less arbitrary assumption that in the long run 80 percent of the property tax reductions would be enjoyed by renters in the form of lower rents and 20 percent by landlords, indicate that only renters with family incomes below $3,500 a year would over the long period have benefited from a shift to his 1 percent income tax. All other family groups would have suffered net losses, ranging from an average of $7 a year at a $5,000 income level to $185 a year at his top income level of $35,000.

These losses, which would have been greater in the year or two following the tax shift, pose a serious problem for the policymaker. In the absence of explicit renter tax relief, the shift to an income tax may encounter widespread opposition; yet it would be no easy matter to design renter reliefs that would bear some reasonable relation to the net tax benefits enjoyed by homeowners.

Difficult as these problems may be, they need not deter greater use of income taxation by any community that regards income as a better measure than property of ability to pay taxes. Alternatively, municipalities that find their expenditures rising faster than their revenues, and there are few that do not these days, can simply decide to finance those increases from a local income tax rather than from higher property tax rates. Special tax relief for renters should not then be a problem, and tax reform is likely to be a good deal easier to achieve.

Effect on Owners of Businesses. The third group distinguished in the Smith study of San Francisco were the owners of businesses located in that city, and one of his most significant, but I think not surprising, findings was that this group would benefit materially from the shift to a local income tax. While businesses would have paid nearly $7 million in 1967 to the city under his 1 percent comprehensive income tax, they would have saved almost $22 million in property taxes, or slightly over half of the total property tax reduction permitted by the enactment of the new income tax. For businessmen such a prospect is bound to be a pleasing one, but it does raise fundamental questions about the role that business taxation should play in local revenue structures. This question will be considered in the next section.

A Local Value-Added Tax

The chief virtue of a local income tax, compared to a general property tax, is its much closer relation to individual abilities to pay for general government services, i.e., services whose benefits are diffused broadly over the whole community and among its inhabitants. Not all local public services, however, are of this kind, a not unimportant portion of them being rendered directly to business enterprises to whom they are just as indispensable as raw materials, or electric and telephone service. By their very nature these local public services, such as fire and police protection, business area parks, and street maintenance and traffic control, cannot be sold to businesses on a unit price basis, and the question then arises as to whether their costs might reasonably be financed by taxation on a benefits-received basis. The first requirement is that the costs of local government services rendered to business be separable, in some acceptable fashion, from the costs of services rendered to the rest of the community. A recent case study for the city of San Leandro, California, done by Peter B. Lund,[2] indicated that while the problems were considerable, detailed activity analysis could provide estimates which the author regarded as sufficiently accurate to serve as the basis for local tax reform.

This much being granted (and studies for other cities are obviously needed), the next question is what specific tax is best suited to defray the costs of local governmental intermediate services to business. It is, of course, impossible to say exactly how much benefit each business receives from local fire and police protection, but the next best thing seems to be to assume that these benefits are more or less closely related to the amount of productive activity that each business enterprise carries out.

If this is the case, a local tax on value added, levied on an origin basis, would be the best form of local business taxation. Such a tax would take as its base the difference between the gross receipts from sales of each resident business and the value of its purchases of goods and services from other businesses, wherever located. In this way the value of productive activity carried out in the taxing jurisdiction itself would be identified and the tax imposed in proportion to it.

It is useful at this point to compare a local value-added tax with the major alternative taxes that could be used to finance city services rendered to business firms.

Comparison with Gross Receipts Tax

A tax on gross receipts would place the same impact burden on firms with the same total sales regardless of the extent to which the productive activity giving rise to those sales occurred within the taxing jurisdiction or elsewhere. Since any government's services benefit only those businesses operating within its jurisdiction, a gross receipts tax would discriminate against those local businesses that purchased a large part of their total product from businesses in other taxing jurisdictions. In addition, a gross receipts tax frequently exempts sales made to purchasers located outside the taxing jurisdiction, and this exemption would be inconsistent with the benefits-received justification of local business taxation.

Comparison with Property Tax

A property tax, of course, is the time-honored benefits-received levy for local governments, the argument being that many of their services are property-oriented and hence are best paid for by a tax on property. While this argument is fine as far as it goes, it does not provide a comprehensive rationale for benefits-received local taxation. Local public services are also people-oriented, and property taxation alone, therefore, may be said to discriminate against capital-intensive businesses and to favor those that are labor-intensive. A value-added tax, in contrast, would treat inputs of capital and labor equally by assessing its charges on the value of output, irrespective of the specific kinds of economic resources used to produce that output.

Comparison with Retail Sales Tax

A retail sales tax is perhaps the least attractive means of benefits-received financing for local governments. In the first place, the high mobility of shoppers within a given metropolitan area prevents independent use of the sales tax by any one jurisdiction in that area to finance a large part of its operations. Secondly, and more important, the rationale of the sales tax, which is to assess its burdens on consumers in proportion to their purchases of taxed output, is quite separate from, and inconsistent with, the rationale of local business taxation, which is to assess each business in proportion to its receipt of local governmental services. Nonretail businesses and businesses selling to nonresidents would be excluded from the retail sales tax base though they clearly enjoy local government services, and taxable businesses would receive no credit for the portion of their total output originating elsewhere, as distinct from the portion that is produced locally with the help of the local government levying the sales tax.

Comparison with Business Income Tax

A business income tax may seem attractive at first glance as a local benefits-received levy. It does, however, have serious weaknesses from this point of view. The most obvious is its exclusion from taxation of all businesses that fail to make a profit in any given year, in spite of the fact that they clearly receive the same benefits from local government operations as do profitable businesses. The underlying distinction here, it must be admitted, is not without its ambiguities. On the one hand, we have those governmental services whose benefits are so widely disseminated that no objective allocation of them can be made to specific people or groups of people. These services, consequently, are best financed by ability-to-pay taxation, and as already noted, a local income tax ranks high for this purpose. On the other hand, we have those local governmental services which can be allocated, more or less objectively, to specific groups of people, but which, for one reason or another, cannot be sold at a price to those groups.

It is these services, insofar as they are rendered to business enterprises, that are under discussion here. Once their existence is accepted, it seems clear that a business income tax is of inadequate scope to finance them equitably. All beneficiaries should pay, regardless of the profitability of their own business operations, and all should pay in as close a relation to the value of benefits received as can be achieved by general business taxation. For this purpose the value-added tax appears to be the leading candidate.

Difficulties in Practice

While attractive in principle, the value-added tax is not without its difficulties in practice, particularly as a means of finance for local governments. It is an unfamiliar tax in this country,[3] and though it is becoming widely used in Europe, it has developed there largely as a broadly-accepted reform of already-existing gross receipts, or turnover, taxes of the cascade variety. Similar justification exists only in a selected number of state and local governments here. Elsewhere the tax merits serious consideration as a means of financing local public services to business, but being a brand new levy, its enactment must clearly be preceded by extensive public discussion and professional analysis. Business groups, for one thing, must be firmly persuaded both of the feasibility of identifying the costs of providing local governmental services to business and of the desirability of financing those costs by value-added tax.

As already stressed, the tax rates high on benefits-received, but not on ability-to-pay, principles. Opponents are quick to note the presumption that value-added tax burdens will be shifted forward to consumers and hence will be characterized by the familiar regressive pattern of the retail sales tax (among families with different amounts of income). This criticism, justified as it is on ability-to-pay grounds, is simply not relevant to a value-added tax used to finance local government services to business. The important equity consideration in this case is the close relation between each firm's value added and its probable receipt of benefits from local government programs. If, as argued above, this relation is closer than that between business public benefits and any other feasible form of local taxation, value-added taxation is the most equitable means of finance available for this purpose. How its burdens may be shifted to workers, consumers, or others is no more relevant than how business costs incurred to purchase labor or supplies are shifted to the same groups.

The most important administrative barrier to the local use of value-added taxation appears to be the allocation of the value added of large interjurisdictional businesses. Value added, however, is made up primarily of profits and payrolls, and much experience in the allocation of these has already been gained in connection with state and local corporate income taxes. Since state enabling legislation would presumably be required before a local government could impose a value-added tax, that occasion could, and should, be used to define a uniform, statewide formula for the allocation of value added among competing local governments. Ideally, of course, this should be done on a nationwide basis so that large businesses become subject neither to the burdens of overtaxation by greedy localities nor to the undeserved favors of undertaxation by governments eager to attract business away from their neighbors.

In any case, there is much to be said for simplicity in the allocation formulas adopted for purposes of local value-added taxation. Since payrolls are reached directly as part of the tax base, profits might be allocated on the basis of property alone. Such a procedure would be the easiest to administer and comply with, and it does not appear to be notably less accurate as a geographical allocator of business profits than the more familiar "Massachusetts" formula based on property, payrolls, and sales.

An Interim Alternative

Indeed, these very considerations suggest a second-best solution to the problem of business taxation that may appeal to local governments unprepared for the early adoption of a value-added tax. This would be to segregate an appropriate part of their already-existing property tax on business and to combine it with a payroll tax so as to simulate as closely as possible the effects of a uniform value-added tax. For example, if property tends to generate profits at a 10 percent rate of return, a 1 percent value-added tax could be approximated by the combination of a 1 percent payroll tax with a 1/10 percent property tax. How close that approximation would be in practice, or what combination of payroll and property tax rates would be best for benefits-received local business taxation, are questions that require, and deserve, empirical investigation. A welcome result of such studies might well be the development of more equitable and efficient local tax systems in this country.

Summary and Conclusions

The general direction of the thrust of new developments in local taxation as it affects business is all too clear. Higher and higher revenues are going to be needed, and local governments show little sign of having either the money or the time needed to design equitable and efficient programs of tax reform and tax increase. It is in this search that businessmen, together with other lay and professional groups, have an increasingly important role to play. This paper has applied the two widely accepted, broad principles of taxation—ability-to-pay and benefits-received—to the task of choosing new sources of local government tax revenue to replace, or at least retard the future growth of, the general property tax.

For ability-to-pay financing it was argued that the personal income tax, carefully integrated with the corresponding state or federal levies, is the leading candidate for increased future use by local governments.

For benefits-received financing of local public services to business enterprises, on the other hand, the leading candidate is the relatively untried value-added tax. Serious study of this levy is accordingly warranted, together with the prospects for simulating its economic effects by a combination of business property and payroll taxes that might be more appealing to local governments, at least over the next few years.

Notes

1. R. Stafford Smith, "Local Income Taxes as an Alternative to Higher Property Taxes: A Summary," *Public Affairs Report* 11 (August 1970), 1-5.
2. Peter B. Lund, "Municipal Costs Arising From Business and Industry: A Case Study of San Leandro, California," (Ph.D. dissertation, University of California, Berkeley, 1967).
3. For detailed economic analyses of the tax see Carl S. Shoup, *Public Finance* (Chicago: Aldine Publishing Company, 1969), and Clara K. Sullivan, *The Tax on Value Added* (New York: Columbia University Press, 1965).

11

Business Appraisal of New Developments in Local Taxation

Lee Hill

Preliminary Definitions

What Is Business?

A business appraisal of new developments in local taxation does not seem to be a particularly ambitious undertaking at first blush. But when one reflects that business has been defined as anything that "occupies the time, attention and labor of men for the purpose of a livelihood or profit,"[1] the potentially limitless scope of the topic emerges.

The corner newsstand is a business as important to its proprietor as the billion-dollar multistate corporation is to its shareholders. In view of the wide diversity of interests in our complex economy, a business appraisal can be made only within a framework of some denominators common to the numerous activities that the term includes. The one most important common denominator is the profit motive.

Therefore, my appraisal of local tax developments will not be a scholar's appraisal, nor an administrator's appraisal, but will be made from the point of view of the impact of local tax developments on business profits. Such an approach does not require disapproval of local taxes generally on the basis that all taxes reduce profits. A tax may be used to provide essential services cheaper or more effectively than business could provide such services for itself, or it may be used to create a favorable business climate, thereby increasing opportunities for profits. Furthermore, it may be desirable for the business to become the tax collector.

What Is Local Taxation?

Local taxes, for the purpose of this discussion, are those taxes levied by a political subdivision deriving its authority from a state. In other words, local taxes are those levied by governmental units below the state level—cities, counties, water districts, school districts, or combinations thereof.

105

What Are New Developments?

A definition of new developments for our framework is more difficult. In a broad sense, the entire field of local nonproperty taxes is a new development. Certainly, the proliferation of local income, payroll, sales, and other excise taxes is generally a post-World War II development. However, these new taxes are symptomatic. The basic new development is that local governments can no longer obtain sufficient funds from traditional sources to meet new or increasing demands for services. The validity of these demands must be appraised, as well as the validity of the taxes levied to satisfy these demands. Some may contend that the new demands cannot be appraised in terms of a profit motive. Refutation of this contention is beyond the scope of this paper. We have stipulated that a business appraisal, if made at all, must be made in terms of a common denominator, which is profits.

How Does Business Appraise Tax Developments Generally?

How does a businessman evaluate a new tax development? Adam Smith formulated the criteria of a good tax in his classic of capitalistic economic theory, *The Wealth of Nations.*[2] He had such insight into the fundamentals that his tests are as valid in today's complex economy as they were when he conceived them 200 years ago. Certainly the clarity and color of Smith's language is striking. Smith said that a tax should be (1) *certain*—as to time, manner, and amount of payment; (2) *convenient*—that is, levied at the time and in the manner in which the taxpayers are best able to pay; and (3) *economical*, that is "contrived as both to take out and to keep out of the pockets of the people as little as possible, over and above what it brings into the public treasury of the state." As for who should pay what amount, Smith thought that taxes should be paid by persons in proportion to the revenues they enjoy under protection of the government—the ability-to-pay doctrine with perhaps a dash of benefits-received thrown in. But Smith was defining a good tax from the viewpoint of a scholar, or of taxpayers in general. The business view is not quite so broad.

How Much Will It Cost?

The first question put to any new tax development by business is "How much will it cost me?" This may be the only question business should ask about a tax development, if cost is considered the excess, if any, of the money detriment from the tax over the value of the benefits derived from the tax. But, in practice, a business will first consider a new development in terms of the actual tax liability without reference to potential benefits. A change in tax liability will be considered in three ways:

First, in absolute terms—how much money?

Second, in comparison with prior period demands—whether there is an increase or decrease in tax liability.

Third, in comparison with the tax liability of other taxpayers and groups of taxpayers.

In determining the actual cost of a new local tax development, the businessman must consider the nature of the tax and his relation to it. Is he a taxpayer or simply a collector of the tax? If the businessman is the taxpayer, he must consider how he can shift the burden of the tax to others and whether such shifting will be through increased prices or through reduced expenditures or dividends. In such shifting, does the burden remain local or is it exported so that persons who reside outside the taxing jurisdiction bear the costs? The question of exporting the tax is of prime interest to business from a competitive point of view, and may be of interest to the taxing authorities from a political point of view.

Compliance costs are of great significance to business, whether as a taxpayer or as a tax collector. These costs include information gathering, reporting, and payment procedures. Administrative complexities and uncertainties can increase these costs until the burden of compliance outweighs the potential penalties resulting from noncompliance. In such a case, there is a great temptation to not pay the tax. The penalties will rise in proportion to the temptation, so that the law first creates the temptation, then ruins those who succumb to it. This violates principles of common sense as well as basic principles of justice.

A disturbing aspect about the administration of local taxes is that in some cases the local administrator does not know how to administer the tax. My company recently received a letter from the administrator of a taxing district concerning the filing and payment procedures in connection with a payroll tax. The administrator stated that he "believed" he was enclosing the correct forms, but that "unfortunately, Mr. _____failed to tell me the necessary information I needed to know relative to this office and I am learning by trial and error." In this situation, it is obvious that the major burden of the tax will fall on those who are most conscientious.

Does It Provide the Needed Revenue
at an Appropriate Cost?

After asking how much a new tax, or altered tax, will cost, business will next ask whether the tax will provide the needed revenue at an appropriate cost to the taxing jurisdiction. This is a practical test, and one particularly appropriate for local taxes. A low-yield, complex tax with high collection costs is an inefficient tax. Such a tax will not satisfy the locality's revenue needs, and the government will be required to enact yet more taxes.

The resources available to local governments are not unlimited. Just as this fact requires ordering or ranking of spending priorities, so it requires maximizing yields through minimizing costs of administering and collecting the tax.

Equity and Fairness

Business will certainly want to view a new development from the point of view of equity and fairness. But I think that a New Jersey judge spoke very realistically about this feature of taxation in the *F. W. Woolworth Company* case several years ago. He said:

Frankly what is fair and unfair in taxation is a vague and uncertain thing. Examination of various decisions reveal the use of such language as "I feel" and "I am of the opinion," etc. Much of the time I feel that most methods of computing taxes are unfair. Generally this feeling depends on the point from which one views the tax, i.e., is it to be paid or collected?[3]

Can business defend an appraisal of local tax developments in terms of its primary interest in profits? Dr. Milton Friedman would probably contend that a corporate executive is not privileged to evaluate taxes in any other way. In a recent article in the *New York Times Magazine*, Dr. Friedman espoused the proposition that the social responsibility of business is to increase its profits. He said:

In a free-enterprise, private-property system, a corporate executive is an employe of the owners of the business. He has direct responsibility to his employers. That responsibility is to conduct the business in accordance with their desires, which generally will be to make as much money as possible while conforming to the basic rules of the society, both those embodied in law and those embodied in ethical custom. . . .

What does it mean to say that the corporate executive has a "social responsibility" in his capacity as businessman? If this statement is not pure rhetoric, it must mean that he is to act in some way that is not in the interest of his employers. . . .[4]

In short, Dr. Friedman seems to be saying that the businessman is morally bound to appraise a tax in the light of the interest of his employers—which invariably is to increase the profits of the business. Certainly, businessmen must meet head-on the all too prevalent view that there is something bad about the pursuit of profits. A blind pursuit of short-term profits may cause temporary injury to the body politic, but it will inevitably ruin the businessman who adopts such a course. The enlightened pursuit of long-term profits in the United States has produced more food, more shelter, more clothing, more abundance for more people than the world has ever before experienced. This enlightened pursuit has not been perfect, nor has it been perfectly applied. But the abundance of goods and services that this imperfect pursuit of profits has produced is the most convincing proof that businessmen must never discard the profit motive as the underlying premise on which they base their actions—including the appraisal of new developments in local taxation.

Tax Developments Follow Demands for
New Governmental Services

To this point, we have examined some of the principles that a businessman will use in appraising a new local tax development in terms of costs. If we now apply these principles to an actual new development, we should be able to complete the cost picture, and, at the same time, bring the benefit side of the business appraisal into focus.

I have already pointed out that new developments in local taxation have a genesis in the many new and competing demands for government services. While time does not permit an appraisal of all these demands, the overall attitude of business will be reflected in an appraisal of the responses local governments are making to the highly publicized demands that immediate action be taken to deal with the transportation problems of inner cities and with the environmental problems.

Some may feel that a discussion of rapid transit and environmental control is not included in the scope of my topic. In my opinion, however, we can better understand and appraise local tax developments by viewing them as devices for providing revenue to solve particular problems. Besides, local tax developments per se appear to be evolutionary rather than revolutionary matters. Many of the developments of the past year or two are extensions of the developments of the past ten years, and as such, are already fixtures in the knowledge and literature of the local tax area. Such topics as (1) the proliferation of local nonproperty taxes, (2) the relatively decreasing but still major significance of the local ad valorem tax, and (3) compliance problems of local income, sales, and other taxes, are already old favorites and were discussed to some extent in the 1964 and 1967 Tax Institute symposiums.[5]

Rapid Transportation

The automobile has improved our lives immeasurably during this century—but at a price. We can examine new local tax developments in terms of one of the problems that putting a large percentage of our population on wheels has caused. In recent years, traffic congestion in cities has become critical. The consequence has been an explosion of demands for immediate and effective solutions. All levels of government are feeling the pressure of urban voters who are concerned about the issue, but the local authorities bear the brunt of the discontent since they are closer to the dissatisfied voters. Undoubtedly, the ultimate solution to these problems requires a unified approach involving all levels of government: federal, state, and local. But a few localities have not been able to await the development of a carefully coordinated plan and are attempting to solve the problem on their own by establishing mass transit systems with such state and federal aid as they are able to secure.

It goes without saying that solving the urban transportation problems will benefit business. Businesses in the currently congested areas will have more employee working time through diminished commuting time, customers will have easier access to stores, and deliveries of goods to and from affected businesses will be accelerated.

Federal participation in satisfying the demands for mass transportation systems has already begun. President Nixon signed into law the Urban Mass Transportation Act of 1970, providing for direct federal participation in solving the need for efficient urban transportation of people and goods. The act authorizes federal grants of $3.1 billion over the next five years for this purpose. But this money is only a fraction of what rapid transit systems will ultimately cost. Part of the cost will come from user fees and part from state and federal grants, but taxes will also be needed. Many people feel that even if user fees *could* cover the cost of the systems, they *shouldn't*. And to the extent a mass transit district levies taxes, the taxes are new taxes for a new need, on top of existing taxes.

Taxes strictly for financing and constructing mass transportation systems are generally occurring only where the area of need covers more than one existing local jurisdiction so that a special purpose governmental unit is formed. Taxing authority has not been granted to all such special purpose districts, some being required to finance the systems through user charges, state or federal grants, or by bonds repayable from earnings of the system.

BART. California has taken the lead in planning and implementing mass transportation systems, having at last count nine separate transit districts. Each district was established by state legislation for one or more counties or parts of counties and the cities and towns included in such districts. The San Francisco Bay Area Rapid Transit District, referred to generally as BART, is the most cited example of a multicounty transportation district. Created in 1957, BART encompasses eighty-four separate units of county, city and county, and city governments.[6] Originally authorized to levy only ad valorem property taxes, the district was recently given authority to levy a sales tax as well.

From the foregoing description, business would have objections to the BART taxes. The creation of a new taxing jurisdiction overlapping eighty-four existing local governments adds one more layer of complexity and administrative burden to local taxation. Such overlapping almost always increases costs to taxpayers.

However, it appears that the BART ad valorem taxes have in fact added a minimum of complexity to tax compliance and administrative burdens. All assessments of value are made for the district by the State Board of Equalization and the county assessors, and the taxes are collected for the district by the tax collectors of the counties included in the district. Only the rate of tax is set by the district's governing body. The county assessors are not burdened with collecting a tax any different from the ad valorem taxes already collected by them for the counties and cities. And since the structure of the preexisting California property tax is embodied in the BART tax, BART does not introduce tax burden distribution problems.

But the ad valorem tax apparently did not do the job. The 1969 California legislature found that the completion of BART was endangered by lack of funds and that "the spiraling increases in property taxes throughout the state are making it more and more difficult for property owners to support the cost of services supplied by local governments."[7] So a new tax was authorized by the state for transit districts, a 1/2 percent "transactions and use" tax administered by the state.[8] Although basically a sales and use tax modeled after the existing California sales tax, the transactions tax differs sufficiently to assure the growth of administrative overburden and taxpayer compliance problems. The increased costs were foreseen by the legislature, and provision was made for the districts to reimburse the state for the administrative costs, including "all preparatory costs including costs of developing procedures, programming for data processing, developing and adopting appropriate regulations, designing and printing of forms, developing instructions for the board's staff and for taxpayers."[9]

How then will business appraise BART? First, profits will be affected least where the local tax contribution to the program is derived from an existing broad-based local tax collected by an existing agency. Second, if a new tax is necessary, it should be broad based and collected by an existing agency.

Southern California Rapid Transit District. The Southern California Rapid Transit District also levies an ad valorem tax and (at least for the rest of 1970) a transactions tax.[10] I offer it as an example of the kind of problems that the creation of a new taxing authority can cause. The district covers most, *but not all*, of Los Angeles County. Compliance and administrative difficulties ring in my head when I read that the geographical reach of the district's taxing power includes that portion of Los Angeles County "lying southerly of the north line of Township 4 North . . . and westerly of the east line of Range 15 West . . . and all that portion of the remainder of said county lying southerly of the north line of Township 2 North. . . ."[11] The State Board of Equalization has supplied a list of the cities and towns included in the district, but with the caveat that the lists "are not certified as to completeness but are the best available unofficial information identifying business and/or mailing destinations within the special transit districts of California as of February 24, 1970." If those charged with administering the taxes can't be sure who's in and who's out, what is the out-of-state businessman supposed to do?

Oregon's Tri-Met District. Oregon last year enacted enabling legislation for mass transit districts.[12] The districts are authorized to raise funds through bonds, user fees, federal grants, and taxes. Authorized taxes include taxes on income or sales (but not on both), and on property, occupations, and payrolls.

The Tri-County Metropolitan Transit District, covering Oregon's three most populous counties, came into being almost immediately. The only tax imposed at present is a 1/2 percent quarterly payroll tax on employers. The tax is administered and collected by the Oregon Department of Revenue.

A frustrating part of the Oregon mass transit legislation is that neither the state nor any Oregon local governments had previously imposed sales taxes or payroll taxes. So although the Tri-Met payroll tax is administered and collected by the State Department of Revenue, the rules, regulations, forms, and other procedures must still be implemented from scratch. The cost of the tax to business is therefore higher than it would have been had the district's taxes piggybacked existing state or local levies.

Another point that business would regard as unfavorable to it is that the Tri-Met chose as its only tax the one authorized tax guaranteed to fall only on business. In fact, the law specifically forbids any pass-through of the tax to employees. Business will undoubtedly benefit from the improved transportation system, but *not* to the exclusion of nonbusiness interests. This violates business' view that taxation should be proportionate to the benefits.

How will Tri-Met score in a business appraisal? Very poorly. It creates a new taxing authority; it levies a new tax never before imposed in the state of Oregon; the tax is levied exclusively on business. Business can approve the administration and collection of the tax by the State Department of Revenue.

Environmental Control

The pollution of the environment lends itself to an even more dramatic presentation than traffic congestion. As in the case of rapid transportation, the federal government is taking an active part in this area. Rapid tax write-offs for pollution control facilities, national standards, and provision of technical expertise to local governments are all being provided.

We had a typical example of local effort in this area in Houston, but the voters of the three counties adjacent to the Houston Ship Channel voted down an ad valorem tax levy which would have been imposed by the Gulf Coast Waste Disposal Authority. The Waste Disposal Authority was created by the Texas legislature in 1969[13] and is, as far as I know, the first multicounty antipollution agency in the state. The authority is charged with the responsibility of taking the necessary action to prevent and abate water pollution and reclaim polluted water for beneficial uses, by means of regional waste disposal systems, regulation of waste disposal, and a regional water quality management program.

The authority is authorized to finance its program through user fees and taxes, and bonds repayable from such fees or taxes. The authority is limited to use of ad valorem taxes, and then only if approved by the voters. The governments of the three constituent counties would collect any taxes levied, but the authority would have its own board of equalization for assessing the value of property.

Applying the same appraisal methods as were used in considering the rapid transit districts, the tax scheme of the Gulf Coast Waste Disposal Authority leaves much to be desired. The new layer of government increases costs to taxpayers. Although the ad valorem tax is already in use by the counties constituting the authority, the use of a new board of equalization rather than the existing county assessment machinery will be expensive because of the duplication of assessment procedures.

Future Systems

An after-the-fact appraisal of the tax consequences of responses by local governments to demands for services is of little practical value unless the lessons learned are reflected in the way future responses are structured. It is far better to influence the future than to complain about the past. Business has not lost all its opportunities in either mass transit or pollution control areas for most of the responses are in the formative stage. But there is no time to waste.

For example, a significant amount of federal money has recently been directed at mass transportation. I feel that this impetus, coupled with the continuing growth of pressure for more efficient urban transportation, will cause a rapid increase in the number of new or improved mass transportation systems proposed around the country. This was made clear to me, at least, when Secretary of Transportation John Volpe recently announced a one-half million dollar grant for a Houston transportation study. I have heard that one proposed Houston mass transportation system would cost up to a billion dollars. As a substantial taxpayer in Houston, my company will be watching the situation and applying, hopefully when and where it will do some good, the same sort of appraisal I have been discussing with you today.

Impact of Business Appraisal on
Local Tax Developments

Will the appraisal by business of new local developments have an effective impact on such developments? Analysis and appraisal, however valid or meritorious, without acceptance accomplishes nothing.

Business Advice Not Sought by Local Governments

Do local governments ask business for its opinion of proposed tax measures? Will local governments listen if business should volunteer unsolicited appraisals? These are critical questions. Unfortunately, past performances do not indicate affirmative answers.

The federal and state governments avail themselves of business advice on matters to a far greater extent than do local governments. The very number of local taxing units complicates the problem immeasurably. Business often does not learn of new local tax developments until they are enacted and in effect.

Now, I believe I have made the point that there are many new developments which will require the imposition of new and increased taxes. At the same time, I believe we do not find that there have been any new or novel developments in local taxation. What we are finding is an aggravation of the old problems of proliferation and pyramiding—with its waste and expense. And we still have the cart before the horse.

Problem of Multiple Jurisdictions

We ought not to have hundreds of taxing jurisdictions in our metropolitan or population centers where one or at least a few political jurisdictions should be employed. Yes, our local jurisdictions must be restructured—just as Leonard Kust stated in his presidential address. But I am rather pessimistic when I make this point as I recognize how little we have accomplished to date in the area of consolidation and metro-type government. Yet statesmen—businessmen, tax administrators, and elected officials—simply must get this show on the road.

We need to establish a forum for the direction and guidance of local taxing jurisdictions in the imposition, enforcement, and administration of taxes. This forum must be composed of both tax administrators and taxpayers. It must be an action forum as our problems are increasing in number and magnitude. Here again there is not much cause for optimism when I consider that fifty taxing jurisdictions (the states) have been struggling for years with the problem of taxation of interstate business. Yet there is a multitude of local taxing jurisdictions to be dealt with in each of the fifty states. Even so, an effective forum of the type suggested seems to me to be the only solution. I am not unmindful of the many organizations which are laboring in this field already—yet the proliferation, pyramiding, and enforcement problems are increasing.

This is a situation that must be faced and remedied. We are involved with new tax problems that can best be solved by the cooperative efforts of all American institutions, including local taxing jurisdictions and the business community. Lines of communication are necessary for effective cooperation and must be established and maintained.

If there ever was a time when innovation and ingenuity are required, the time is now. For there seems to have been an alarming erosion of the American notions that government should be maintained as closely as possible to the people and that local governments should assume responsibility for local problems. Surely, this is the time for business to consider and appraise local governments and their tax structures and to place its skills and talents at the disposal of local governments to the end that our problems shall be solved in the context of a free enterprise society.

Notes

1. Sargent Land Co. v. Von Baumbach, 242 U.S. 503 (1917).
2. Adam Smith, *The Wealth of Nations*, Book V, Chapter II, Part II.
3. F.W. Woolworth Co. v. Director of Division of Taxation, 45 N.J. 466, 213 A.2d 1 (1965).
4. Milton Friedman, "The Social Responsibility of Business Is to Increase Its Profits," *New York Times Magazine*, September 13, 1970, p. 33.
5. See *State and Local Taxes on Business* (Princeton: Tax Institute of America, 1965); *Federal-State-Local Fiscal Relationships* (Princeton: Tax Institute of America, 1968), especially Part Five: "State and Local Fiscal Responsibility Versus Tax Compliance Simplicity for Interstate and Interlocal Business"; and L.L. Ecker-Racz, *The Politics and Economics of State-Local Finance* (Englewood Cliffs, N.J.: Prentice-Hall, Inc., 1970).
6. California Pub. Util. Code §§ 28500-29757.
7. California Stats. 1969 Ch. 24, §1, noted under Calif. Pub. Util. Code §29140.
8. Calif. Rev. & Tax. Code §§7251 et seq.
9. Calif. Ref. & Tax. Code §7272.
10. Calif. Pub. Util. Code §§ 30000-31520.
11. Calif. Pub. Util. Code §30100.
12. Chapter 643, Oregon Laws 1969, ORS ¶267.010 et seq.
13. VATS Art. 7621d-a.

12

Policy Considerations in Designing Local Tax Structures

Robert F. Steadman

It is a great pleasure to be a part of this symposium on a subject of grave importance to this country. It is presumed that my presence is due to the fact that the Committee for Economic Development, with which I am associated, has issued a number of policy statements within the last five years that bear directly upon policy considerations in designing local tax structures. By and large, what I have to say will be drawn from official pronouncements by the Research and Policy Committee of CED. Wherever I depart from these positions, I shall try conscientiously to identify those points that are my individual and personal responsibilities.

Role of Committee for Economic Development

For the benefit of those who are not fully familiar with the character of CED, perhaps I should quite briefly explain the nature of its interest. The Committee for Economic Development was formed in 1942 by a group of outstanding public leaders and distinguished economists, with the object in mind of developing policies for adoption by the national government that would be appropriate to secure a transition from wartime to peacetime conditions without the grave dislocations feared by many citizens. That project bore fruit, through the work of 3,000 local community committees formed to assure a satisfactory transition, and through adoption by the national government of the Employment Act of 1946 and other legislation designed to gain the desired result.

Over the intervening years, CED has continued to develop and publish statements on national policy intended to gain public support for solutions deemed most appropriate to the needs of the times. The great majority of our 200 trustees are leaders in the various fields of American business, with a minority of university presidents.

CED has two characteristics unusual among organizations working in this field. First, it calls upon the most distinguished academicians and experts in each field examined, so that members of the academic fraternity sit jointly with committees of CED trustees in a search for agreement in the light of factual data and the good judgment of experienced and distinguished citizens. Second, CED

117

emphasizes its concern for the general or public interest, as opposed to any effort to defend or advocate the special interests of the corporations or industries or economic groups whose leaders join in these discussions. The thesis is that a healthy economy in a stable society will provide a social and economic climate in which well managed business enterprise may flourish while the personal satisfactions to be gained from an attractive quality of life may be enhanced.

CED Policy Statements

Every policy statement issued by CED is considered and approved by its Research and Policy Committee. That committee is directed in our bylaws to:

Initiate studies into the principles of business policy and of public policy which will foster the full contribution by industry and commerce to the attainment and maintenance of high and secure standards of living for people in all walks of life through maximum employment and high productivity in the domestic economy.

In the years following World War II, most of CED's policy statements dealt with economic issues—involving fiscal policy, monetary policy, foreign trade, economic growth and productivity, and the like. In recent years it has become more and more obvious, however, that the well-being of the national economy is heavily dependent upon the capacity and responsiveness of government at all levels—national, state, and local. Without competent and effective government capable of putting sensible proposals into practice, the economic objectives of CED can hardly be achieved.

It was for this reason that CED established a special Committee for Improvement of Management in Government in 1963. This committee has prepared a number of policy statements aimed at correction of many deficiencies in the federal government itself, with respect to personnel, budgeting, and the operations of Congress. But the documents dealing with the modernization of local and state governments bear most directly on the subject under consideration.

CED's policy statement on *Modernizing Local Government*, issued in July of 1966, placed heavy stress on the need for local self-government. To quote: "Our fundamental concern is that every community in the nation be capable of effective management of its local affairs." At the same time, CED's finding of fact was that the existing patterns of local government fell short of the great and growing needs facing both urban and rural America. Most of our 80,000 local governments are too small to function well in the provision of community services; most of them lack the broad legal authority necessary to respond to complex issues; the overlapping layers so common in this country handicap and limit each level in tackling large issues; and the internal organization of many forms of local government does not meet the reasonable standards set by persons familiar with modern organizational structures.

CED has taken a strong position, also, in support of changes in all three branches of state government—executive, legislative, and judicial—that would permit the states to function more ably. These views were set forth in *Modernizing State Government*, issued in July of 1967.

Many of the recommendations made in these two policy statements have a direct bearing upon local taxation. Moreover, a third statement issued in June, 1967, under the title *A Fiscal Program for a Balanced Federalism*, is more clearly and directly in point.

Perspectives on Local Finance

To see the relationship between these statements of policy on modernization of state and local governments or intergovernmental fiscal relations and local tax structures more clearly, some perspectives concerning local government finance will be useful.

Magnitude of Local Expenditures

Over one-quarter of all direct expenditures by governments in this country are made by local units ($82 billion out of $308 billion in 1968-1969). When we exclude social security and other trust accounts, 29 percent of all "general expenditures" by governments are made by local units ($73.5 billion out of $256 billion in 1968-1969). By any measure, the direct local expenditures are much larger—by more than half again as much—than those of the states.

Inadequacy of Local Tax Revenues

However, taxes levied by local units provide less than half of local expenditures or local revenues ($34.8 billion out of $71.9 billion in general revenues in 1968-1969). Grants-in-aid from state and federal governments came to $26.1 billion in that year, and this source of funds is growing far more rapidly than local tax revenues. Charges and miscellaneous general revenues account for most of the balance of local revenues—$11.1 billion in 1968-1969.

Ratio of Local to Total Tax Collections

The grand total of all local taxes is only about 15.6 percent of the grand total of taxes levied by governments in the United States ($34.8 billion out of $222.7 billion in 1968-1969). Yet, local taxation receives more public attention and creates more resistance than much heavier levies imposed by state and federal governments.

Heavy Reliance on Property Taxes

Property taxes account for the lion's share of all local levies. They were $29.7 billion in 1968-1969, compared with $1.4 billion of individual income taxes and $2.5 billion in sales and gross receipts taxes. All other tax sources yielded only $1.2 billion. The cities, particularly the larger cities, account for nearly all of the income and sales taxes. Counties, townships, and school districts depend almost exclusively upon the property tax.

State-Local Fiscal Relationships

In any rational discussion of the subject it is impossible to separate local tax policy considerations from those of the states. State-local fiscal relationships are so valid and so intimate that separation is a practical impossibility. This is shown clearly by two facts derived from the Bureau of the Census's publication *Governmental Finances in 1968-69*. Local governments in this country outspent the states in direct expenditures, $82 billion to $49 billion. But, in general revenues from their own sources, the states took in more money than the local units of government, $50 billion to $46 billion. In other words, the states use their taxing powers, supplemented by federal aids to the states, to sustain the delivery of local services.

CED Policy Statements on Local Finance

These facts form the background for a series of CED policy positions concerning local finance, ranging from the general to the specific. Some of these may be stated as follows.

Transfer of Welfare Burdens

First, the burdens involved in public welfare administration should be lifted from the local units of government, and from the states as well. In the policy statement issued in April of 1970, *Improving the Public Welfare System*, CED gave its support to the main principles in President Nixon's Family Assistance Plan, with a number of qualifications and extensions. But CED went well beyond any short-term solution in its recommendation that the federal government should set as a goal the takeover of all state and local public assistance costs over the next five years. Further, CED proposes assumption by the federal government, at that time, of responsibility for administration of the public assistance function.

Greater State Responsibility for Education

Second, CED has recommended in *A Fiscal Program for a Balanced Federalism* (June, 1967) that the states should take greater responsibility for the function of education, either through direct expenditures or grants-in-aid, in order to help equalize and improve the financial ability of local governments to meet their needs in this field. There is increasing dissatisfaction with the actual operation of the formulas upon which state aid to the public schools is based in many if not most of the states.

It comes as a shock to learn that suburban schools with large taxable resources per pupil actually receive larger amounts of state aid than are paid to city school systems that care for much larger percentages of disadvantaged children. I must offer this as my personal opinion, above and beyond any statement of policy issued by CED, but I believe that there is a powerful trend of thought in the direction of outright state assumption of full responsibility for financing the whole system of public education in America.

If these two great and primary functions of government and responsibility for their support are shifted from state and local to federal government in the case of public welfare and from state and local to sole state responsibility in the case of public education, then an enormous burden would be lifted from the sphere of local taxation. In 1968-1969 the total local burden for education, in addition to grants-in-aid, was $20 billion, and the state-local shares of public welfare payments, combined, came to nearly $6 billion—a figure that has risen rapidly since June of 1969.

Abolition of Personal Property Taxation

Third, CED has taken a strong position against the use of personal property taxation, at least at the local level, as distinct from the taxation of real property. The absurdity of any effort to assess fairly the household effects of families either urban or rural has been quite evident for more than fifty years.

The pernicious effects of efforts to assess and tax business inventories and equipment is equally evident. Private enterprise should not be forced into dubious inventory policies of dubious merit in order to minimize this kind of tax. The costs of compliance are often high, as in the case of the Great Atlantic and Pacific Tea Company maintaining a monthly inventory account for its stores separately located in some thousands of local taxing districts.

The communities that tax modern equipment do injury to their own growth prospects, since public policy should encourage the installation of the most efficient possible means of production rather than penalize or handicap its most progressive establishments.

Application of personal property taxation to livestock and modern farm equipment has the same kind of injurious effect upon agriculture as similar levies on inventories and equipment have upon business concerns. Of course, local efforts to levy personal property taxes on intangibles were found to be inappropriate long ago, and have generally been abandoned. Yet, state statutes and constitutions continue to impose archaic, unworkable requirements in the whole field of personal property taxation.

Personal property taxation by local units of government should be eliminated, just as quickly as the legal changes can be made. Four states (Delaware, Hawaii, New York, and Pennsylvania) exempt personal property from assessment and taxation. Nationwide, personal property assessments amounted to less than 15 percent of all taxable local assessment rolls, and abandonment of this revenue source would have serious financial impact in few jurisdictions. This would be most clearly the case if the costs of education and public welfare were transferred to the states and federal government at the time this change is made.

Improvement in Real Property Tax Administration

Fourth, the administration of the real property tax requires drastic improvement in the vast majority of local jurisdictions. Many authorities are critical of the regressive effects of property taxation, but such effects would be greatly reduced if this tax were based upon equitable and accurate assessments. In *Modernizing Local Government* CED made the following observation:

Real property tax administration suffers from two major sources of inequity: unequal assessment and under-assessment. In view of the primary reliance on real property taxes, it is quite shocking that in most parts of the country—whether urban or rural—its administration may be accurately described as inequitable, inefficient, incompetent, or corrupt. There is no more vivid illustration of the need for reform of local institutions.[1]

Since that statement was issued in 1966, the Bureau of the Census has isssued a new report entitled *Taxable Property Values*. This report shows that in 1,401 selected areas, located in all fifty states, barely half of these 1,400 areas had coefficients of intra-area dispersion for nonfarm houses less than 20.0, during 1966. Moreover, the Bureau of the Census reports that in terms of measurable sales of ordinary real estate in 1966, the average assessed value of all residential properties, nationwide, was 34.9 percent. For commercial and industrial properties, the ratio was nearly the same—33.9 percent. But vacant lots were assessed, on the average, far below that level, at only 24.1 percent. And acreage and farms were valued still lower, at 17.8 percent, which is only about half the ratio for residential, commercial, and industrial properties. Real estate developers and speculators gain great financial advantage from this situation, not justified by any benefit gained by the community at large.

Reduction in Number of Local Units

CED has strongly recommended a sharp reduction in the number of local governments operating within this country. This point has direct relevance to property assessment. There are about 18,000 primary assessment jurisdictions in this country, many of them much too small to permit the employment of professional assessors. In many cases assessors are elected officials, although direct election is never the right way to select personnel with technical or professional assignments. To quote again from *Modernizing Local Government:*

Most of the injustice and waste under the present system could be eliminated—quite readily—if property tax administration were entrusted to strong local units, properly organized and managed. Small, overlapping tax assessment and collection districts, with their amateur elective assessors and collectors, must give way to professionally competent personnel under incorruptible supervision. These changes would produce sizable administrative savings, permit equitable and accurate property valuations, and eventually reduce the number of successful assessment appeals. State governments have a basic responsibility even though they gain little revenue from property taxes. They should set assessment standards, inspect enforcement, and provide technical assistance upon request. . . .

When county governments are reconstituted, they should be entrusted with property tax administration—at least for an initial trial period—under state supervision and with state technical assistance. Modernized local governments should be given authority to use a variety of additional tax sources.[2]

Unless local assessment systems can be modernized and made to function properly in terms of simple justice, then the state governments should follow the example of Hawaii and assume direct state responsibility for valuation of all taxable properties. Incidentally, I would offer another personal observation at this point: If the states do assume full financial responsibility for public education, it would not be inappropriate for the states to levy statewide taxes on all real property in support of this function, in order to achieve equity and uniformity within each state.

Permissive Taxation for Larger Local Units

Fifth, the authority of local units of government, most particularly those in the larger urban centers, to levy taxes other than upon property should not be withheld by state legislators. CED has recommended, however, that local taxes on incomes or upon sales and gross receipts should not be levied independently, but should be applied only in addition to existing state taxes upon such objects. This could properly be described as a piggyback approach, and is coming into more general use.

CED stated its preference for taxation of personal incomes by the states, and has proposed that liberal credits against federal income taxes should be granted in order to encourage universal use by the states of this form of taxation. This arrangement, together with a restructuring of categorical grants-in-aid along more rational lines, is considered by CED to be far preferable to any system of revenue sharing without strings or limitations of any kind. It is my personal opinion that gifts from the Treasury to the states and their local units of government—even when at some time in the distant future there are federal revenues to spare for this purpose—might have a most unfortunate effect through shoring up and sustaining patterns of state and local government that require internal improvement. In other words, these gifts would tend to delay the correction of obvious defects that call for major and urgent reforms. If the federal government does adopt a system of revenue sharing, I would hope that it would be made conditional upon the construction of a far better system of local government than is found in most parts of this country.

Conclusion

The changes in the patterns of taxation by state and local governments that have been proposed by CED were designed to serve the best interests of all the people in our local communities, states, and the nation. They have been offered, of course, in the belief that the legitimate interests of business enterprise would also be well served. We need tax systems that encourage economic growth and enhance human productivity; we should not tolerate systems antagonistic to these goals. Assurance of just laws equitably and competently administered would add enormously to this nation's faith in its own great future.

Notes

1. Committee for Economic Development, Research and Policy Committee, *Modernizing Local Government* (New York, 1966), p. 54.
2. Ibid., p. 55.

13 Discussion of Local Taxation of Business

Chairman George K. Dunn, *Zenith Radio Corporation:* The time has now come for questions and discussion.

Mr. Arnold Cantor, *AFL-CIO:* Just a very specific question: In concerning yourself with the problems of the renters, you noted that the low-income groups tend to be better off in substituting an income for a property tax; and that the difference to the higher income groups is somewhat marginal, but on balance they would pay quite a bit more. How does the federal tax deductibility feature enter into it? Wouldn't that be enough to swing it the other way?

Professor George F. Break, *University of California, Berkeley:* I know they incorporated the federal tax deductibility for homeowners. I am not sure about renters. The question is to what extent the local income tax paid by renters would be deductible from their federal income tax base when, and if, they itemize deductions. Now, I would guess that many people in those income brackets would be taking the standard deduction. The federal standard deduction has been increased substantially, or will be, and so then deductibility of local taxes will not matter in a very large number of low- and middle-income families.

Mr. Cantor: No, but you mentioned brackets up to $35,000.

Professor Break: Those figures I gave you took that deductibility into account for homeowners. As I say, I am not sure what the answer is for renters. And remember that these calculations assume that 80 percent of the property tax reduction was reflected in lower rents. If you want to take the other extreme and say there is no reduction in rents, then all renters are going to be worse off by simply the amounts of local income tax to which they are subject.

Mr. Sidney Glaser, *New Jersey Division of Taxation:* If a local municipality were to adopt an income tax, to what extent do you think the enabling legislation should limit the municipality? Do you think the enabling legislation should contain all the details of an ordinance, or do you think just the broad terms would be sufficient?

Professor Break: I think the enabling legislation ought to define the base for the income tax so that every jurisdiction uses the same base, and it ought to solve the problem of commuters. That is to say, in deciding who is going to get to tax that income, whether the jurisdiction in which they work or the jurisdiction in which they live; or whether maybe it is split evenly between the two so that you don't get multiple taxation of mobile taxpayers; but I would personally prefer to leave the rate open. It seems to me if you set a ceiling rate, you are very likely to find that that is the rate everywhere, and I would prefer to let communities set their own rates. I don't think they will abuse the privilege, particularly in urban areas, because of the competition.

Mr. Gerald D. Hall, *New Jersey State Chamber of Commerce:* Professor, I have to remark that it seems to me your graduate student who examined the effects of the tax in the Bay area deluded himself when he convinced himself that business was going to suffer some benefits from this because, first of all, it would appear to be the history of municipal income taxes that they are not levied for tax relief, but that they have been imposed to meet very necessary fiscal requirements of a particular time and crisis.

Second, certainly business would be faced with an immediate demand that its workers be held harmless and that compensating pay raises accompany the tax.

Professor Break: Well, I think you may be deluding yourself on the first question. I think, in fact, that if an income tax is adopted, it does tend to take the place of higher property taxes that otherwise would have had to be collected. This, at least, is the finding of a 1967 Tax Foundation study of *City Income Taxes*.

Your second comment does raise a very interesting question about wage rates. It seems to me that if San Francisco, for example, were to levy an income tax, businesses would very likely find the cost of secretaries going up—using secretaries as an example of a type of worker that is pretty mobile. They might well have to pay their secretaries and other mobile workers sufficiently more for them to pay the local income tax, assuming that commuters were subject to the tax.

I doubt that business executives are quite that mobile. I doubt that companies would have to pay them any more because I don't think they would readily move out of San Francisco to avoid the local income tax; but certain groups of workers would and could. I don't know the answer to how much of an income tax increase gets into union bargaining and gets into high wages that way. I doubt it myself, but I can't prove it one way or the other.

Mr. Leonard E. Kust, *Cadwalader, Wickersham and Taft:* Professor Break, if you are going to move to a benefits-received justification for a tax on business, why not go all the way and try to convert the tax structure to a user charge system? It seems to me there are certain psychological and even rhetorical advantages in calling them user charges, and if you can develop a technique for identifying the local and city services that are attributable to the whole business community, won't those same techniques perhaps permit you to identify how much is attributable to each business as a user charge?

Professor Break: Well, my thought was that while you can say what the cost of services going to a certain area in the city is, you cannot say what the cost of services going to certain individual businesses in that area is. I think if you have a nicely defined business community that occupies a certain area, you can probably say what it costs the city to provide police and fire protection, and to maintain the streets and parks in that area. I doubt that you can say how much an individual business enjoys those benefits so that you could levy a user charge on it. So my thought was that you just take the total cost of providing those services to that area, and you collect it by means of a value-added tax on the businesses. That amounts to assuming that each of them enjoys those benefits in proportion to the productive activities it carries out. The more productive activity, the more benefit it gets.

This is an assumption. I don't know of any better one to use, but I would certainly expand the use of user charges where you can identify the benefits. I doubt that you can here.

Dr. Lloyd E. Slater, *New York State Deputy Commissioner for Tax Research:* Professor Break, there is a basic assumption on your part that I want to challenge, but I want to get around to a specific part of it only. From an economic point of view, of course, you haven't considered the providing of a market or place to work as something that would be subject to your user charges. In the East, at least, where we have made heavy use of income taxes at the state level and for certain cities—both on personal and business incomes—we are convinced it would not be economically possible to have done it if we had not taxed the nonresident individuals who work within the area. I want to get back to that one, and that is my principal point.

I also want to say that we have moved more and more to the thought that we have to adjust our taxes on business so that they are heavily weighted in relation to marketing and away from the point of manufacturing if in the long run we are going to be able to attract a sufficient amount of manufacturing to provide the necessary basic productivity on which the rest of our total society can exist.

Now I realize that economists differ greatly, and I assume your school of thought is different from mine. Personally I don't feel the economic considerations here are the proper ones. So I would rather not challenge the economics. I would rather look only at the practical political consequences and say that now that we have been working with these taxes over a long period we are convinced that the only way we can have state and local taxes that will not have an unbearable economic effect is to arrange it somehow so that all competitors, in competing either for jobs or for market, have to pay the same tax.

I would like to make a special point of something that I am very much concerned about at the moment, because there is some federal legislation that is part way through the Congress and about to go the rest of the way through that would begin to take away—and almost certainly would eventually lead to taking away fully—the opportunity to tax nonresidents. We are convinced that if this should occur the economic effect of making it possible for somebody to move outside and still have the same job would be so serious that the exodus of higher income persons that has already been very serious in our cities would further increase. These people have been replaced, unfortunately, by the very poor so that we already are having such great difficulties, both at the central city level and at the level of the states in which those cities are located, that we must have some more help from the federal government. At the moment we are faced with the possibility of the federal government being about to enact something that will make it almost impossible for us to continue to have the fiscal capacity even that we presently have.

Now I would hate to have any thought develop here that we could continue to have local income taxes if we were unable to tax nonresidents, particularly in the face of the present situation in which I am going to be next week of trying every way I can to get the people at the state and local level to pressure Congress to keep this particular legislation from going through. I am firmly convinced that we couldn't continue to have local income taxes. I would like to have you comment on this.

Professor Break: You have raised a great many complex questions. I am afraid I can't possibly answer them here, even if I could remember all of them.

My ideal plan for local financing, as I think I indicated, would have only a local income tax on residents to finance schools. No income tax on business to finance schools locally at all. If there is a tax for education on business, I think it ought to be statewide. The only tax on business would be for the services that I think they do receive, financed by the value-added tax.

Now that is, I admit, a very drastic change in our present tax system, and I don't expect it to emerge quickly, if ever. As part of that plan, I would certainly move all welfare expenditures to the federal government as fast as I could get them there, and that includes all assistance to low-income families, special education cost, plus training, income maintenance, and the whole thing. I think that would do a good deal to help solve the financial problems of the central cities.

In the meantime, I understand that you have to find the revenue. I have no objection to a local income tax that includes commuters' earnings.

Dr. Slater: Thank you.

Professor Don M. Soule, *University of Kentucky:* Mr. Hill, based on your description of what you say is the necessary business reaction to taxation—whatever is legal, whatever will increase profit—are we correct in assuming that this is also the position of business in environmental control and pollution? In other words, anything that is legal and will increase profit is, therefore, proper?

Mr. Lee Hill, *Humble Oil & Refining Company:* Yes. I think we have a responsibility in the tax area. I think we have a responsibility in the environmental area. I think it is most important that we do our part. I think that this matter of profits and how you shift these costs is our big problem. It is not the theory of the profits, it seems to me, and not the theory of our being involved in these areas. It's the methods that we use in shifting these costs around.

Chairman Dunn: Are there any other questions?

Mr. Victor E. Ferrall, *American Telephone and Telegraph Company:* I can't pass this opportunity to ask my good friend, Lee Hill, a question at a time when, as he has indicated, he finds himself completely surrounded by professors and tax administrators, especially since my question is highly theoretical, and I know how Lee likes those. It is theoretical in the sense that it has just come to me as I have been sitting here yesterday and this morning listening.

Those of us that have sat on municipal governing bodies have worked on local budgets—which, incidentally, is a long and dismal procedure. As we went through each of those budgets, we identified some items that had to be increased and some that could be decreased—with the inevitable effect on the tax rate that we knew would be the consequence of each increase or decrease. Also, as we hark back to that experience, we can identify certain of the items that—to tie in with Len Kust's question—would have been susceptible to a tax that was something in the nature of a user fee.

Now, suppose that with experience like that with local budgets in mind, we were to list, with some practical reality, the expenditures that states as well as local governments must make—then, with that list in mind, move into the controversial area of taxation of interstate businesses, on which there is still much rather bitter disagreement. Instead of the attempt now being made to resolve this conflict on the basis of jurisdiction to apply this or that kind of tax, suppose that Congress, at our behest and in the exercise of its power to regulate interstate commerce, were to say to the states: Here is a set of a limited number of taxes. Here is the nature of each tax and its allowable base. If a state applies any of these taxes to interstate business on a statewide basis, with allocation of the tax to local governments left to the state, that state will not be considered guilty of having put an undue burden on interstate commerce. If, on the other hand, a state attempts to apply other taxes it will be considered as having imposed an unfair burden. Perhaps—to take Lloyd Slater's problem into consideration—a part of one of the permissible taxes on business could be passed through to employees, both resident and nonresident.

What do you think of that as a highly theoretical possibility?

Mr. Hill: I think that that is possible. I think that we may have to become more arbitrary in this area than I would want to see. I hate for the state or local subdivisions to be hamstrung in what they can do. I like for there to be some flexibility in one area, being able to impose one type of tax, and in another area to impose a different type of tax. But I do feel that in this interstate area we probably will finally end up with some fairly arbitrary rules, and I think that is the point you are making. I think we probably will.

Mr. James C. Saylor, *Philadelphia Electric Company:* You mentioned piggybacking the sales tax, for instance. I think that is a step in the right direction. However, it creates difficulty for an organization that is making sales in many jurisdictions. Would it not be possible to do the same thing by having a credit against the state tax for the local taxes so you would be paying only state taxes?

Dr. Robert F. Steadman, *Committee for Economic Development:* In Virginia the state does collect the sales tax. All the county does is pass a resolution saying: We take advantage of this option, and we levy this additional 1 percent tax, whereupon the state collects it in every retail jurisdiction in the area and returns that amount. It is simple as can be once you have the state system.

Mr. Saylor: You have a different rate on various sales in various jurisdictions in the state, right?

Dr. Steadman: Yes, although most of the counties have taken advantage of the option.

Mr. Saylor: So the tax collector, the person that is selling the goods in more than one of these areas, has to know the rates in all these areas?

Dr. Steadman: Oh, yes.

Mr. Saylor: What I am suggesting is that they just have one rate for the state, and the local tax be a credit against the state tax, so that the rate of the state tax would have to fluctuate each year, depending upon the local levies. I think the same thing could be accomplished.

Dr. Steadman: Or you could do it by just raising the tax and then adding the extra cent and distributing it back on some formula basis. This can be done, too, but we like the idea of having the local authority either raise it or not. Actually, every county in the whole metropolitan area and every urban county in Virginia has taken advantage of the extra penny.

Mr. Saylor: But the local jurisdiction should have the responsibility for deciding whether they want the tax.

Dr. Steadman: Right.

Mr. Saylor: So just putting a state rate on and allocating it, I don't think is the solution.

Dr. Steadman: No.

Dr. Slater: May I comment on that? The problem is, of course, that from the point of view of the city, that would be fine. From the point of view of the rest of the people in the state, they would be contributing to statewide expenses in a different way than the cities would be that had taken over the revenue. Now the practical effect, of course, would be politically that every locality would, under this circumstance, protect itself by enacting a local tax, and the state would have no revenue left.

Part IV:
The Impact of Political Considerations in Shaping State and Local Taxes on Business

At an earlier session we heard several points of view on state and local tax systems and business tax components. These covered the range from studies of long-term objectives to current practical administrative aspects of the subject.

In achieving a balanced tax program, we all have reservations on accomplishment as was typified in comments by John Shannon supporting his position that a state's responsibility for tax reform does not end by achieving full value assessment.

Very practical political considerations come into play in shaping the desired tax system. Do we get there? And how do we get there? So it is now appropriate to examine the political aspects of enacting tax laws affecting business.

Robert C. Plumb

Director of Taxes, American Cyanamid Company, and Chairman of Thursday Luncheon Session

14

Political Considerations in Shaping the Tax Structure of Business

W. Russell Arrington

At the outset let me commend the Tax Institute of America, and particularly those of you who set the tone and selected the topics for this important and impressive symposium. Your agenda is comprehensive, unusually thoughtful, and timely.

Your emphasis this morning on the *quality* of the tax structure we impose upon business is especially commendable. A quality tax structure implies, by definition, an *equitable* tax structure—one that is fair to all taxpayers.

It will come as no surprise to this audience that there are people in America who are suspicious of businessmen, and particularly of the attitude of business-men toward taxation. It is a suspicion born of looking at American history from one point of view, a view that businessmen do not look beyond their own self-interest in discussing taxation. I believe your emphasis on quality will help to shatter that myth—the myth that for men of business the only fair tax is the one they do not pay!

I stand before you with impeccable credentials to shatter a few myths myself on the subject of my remarks: the political considerations in shaping the taxa-tion of business. And I have come by my credentials the hard way. For twenty-five years I publicly asserted to my constituents that so long as I was a member of the General Assembly there would never be a state income tax in Illinois if I had my way.

Well, we have an income tax in Illinois today, and I was its chief sponsor. I could explain to my constituents that my virtuous position against a state in-come tax was simply overwhelmed by the capricious turn of the public mood. If that argument didn't wash with the voters, I could simply say that I fought the good fight, but that, in the end, the forces of evil—and the Democrats—had the votes. I could say that I would continue to oppose fiscal maniacs at every turn, and that I would never surrender to the venal politicians who rifle the wallets and pocketbooks of citizens and taxpayers.

Language like that can generate a few votes. But in my case it would be a problem. Anyone familiar with Illinois politics in 1969 would nail me in the question-and-answer period. They would want to know *why*—in view of the re-marks I made earlier in my political career—I turned up in 1969 as the chief sponsor of the income tax.

The only honest way I can respond to a question about my sponsorship of

135

the Illinois income tax is with the opening sentence of a now famous book with which many of you are undoubtedly familiar. *The Money Game* was written in 1967 by a New York stockbroker who began his commentary on the secret life of Wall Street with the statement: "The world is not the way they tell you it is."

That statement could serve as well for an introduction to a book on Illinois politics.

The passage of the Illinois income tax, with a corporate differential, came about not because political considerations were ignored. On the contrary, it was because one set of political considerations prevailed over a less compelling set. My mail ran heavily against passage of the tax. There was very little written in favor of passage. But at the same time there was mountainous mail demanding more funds for education, mental health, and highways.

The voters who demanded more funds and better services had to be weighed against those who opposed the income tax, even though very few of the first group suggested an income tax as a way of generating the funds they demanded. One of the tribulations of elected office is reading letters from and listening to constituents who can be eloquent in their demands for service—and eloquently silent on the subject of how the revenue for those services should be provided.

In the end, one makes a calculated guess that a portion of those demanding a service will accept the increased taxation necessary to provide it. Nearly all tough political questions are resolved in this manner, by weighing one set of political considerations against another.

In the brief time available to me I cannot cover even a small number of the political considerations which affect the taxation of business. Instead, permit me to dwell on three that strike me as especially significant. Also permit me to address myself to those considerations by asking you three—I hope somewhat provocative—questions:

1. What influence do campaign contributions from certain businesses have on the way those businesses are taxed?
2. What influence does economic ignorance in an elected legislator have on the way we tax business?
3. How does the pressure to achieve social reform affect the taxation of business?

The first of these questions I would categorize as having diminished in importance. The second is a chronic and frustrating one. The third is developing as one of the most significant political considerations in the taxation of business.

Campaign Contributions

It will come as no surprise that state legislators tend to look sympathetically upon the requests of those who have contributed to their campaigns. But I submit to you the proposition that in the legislature I know best, the one here in Illinois, those legislators who can be called—in newspaper parlance—"captives of a special interest group," are an *insignificant minority*. There is no interest group in Illinois, from insurance companies to the people who represent the interests of retarded children, that is able to influence significantly the course of legislation by contributing to political campaigns.

In the days when state legislators in Illinois rode to Springfield on horseback things may have been different. News traveled at the same pace as the horse. Most voters did not know what happened in Springfield until the session was over. A resourceful lobbyist in 1845 might have been able to circulate enough cash and enough promises of future favors to influence a roll call. That is impossible today.

Business in Illinois provides the bulk of campaign contributions. If campaign contributions had significantly influenced tax policy in Illinois, we would not have passed an income tax in Illinois in 1969.

The era of "protectionism" in tax policy, a policy in which campaign contributions played a significant part, has reached very nearly the end of its rope in American politics. We will continue to have "pockets of protectionism" in our tax structure. We will continue to have "tax shelters." But the *people* will demand that when these age-old devices are used, those who advocate their use do so for the welfare of everyone.

Legislative Ignorance

Legislative ignorance is another matter. I have always felt that fiscal matters are those least understood by the majority of legislators. Social issues like crime, education, and mental health are, comparatively speaking, easily grasped.

What then is the impact of sheer economic ignorance on fiscal policy? Does ignorance favor business, or is the ignorance responsible for the defeat of legislation because some senator labels it "fat cat"? My own feeling is that "fat cat" speeches do influence some votes often enough to be considered "political considerations." The point to be made is that ignorance of fiscal matters leaves the average legislature sensitive to the "fat cat" charges of the demagogue—and that one key element in reducing political considerations in tax policy is *better education* of the average legislator in fiscal matters.

In recent years there can be discerned increasing efforts on the part of individual legislators to inform themselves on the financial structure and operation of state government. This has been compelled by the hugely increasing cost of government in response to which the legislator is asked to provide the additional funding.

The most conspicuous recent example here in Illinois is the one I have already alluded to: namely, the new Illinois income tax. That measure was passed by a substantial majority of the members of both political parties, in the Senate at least. The individual legislator supporting such legislation was required to become convinced that the state and local governments needed large additional funding, and that an income tax was the only source which could provide these funds.

Very recently, the people of our state voted favorably on the legislative proposal that the personal property tax on individuals be abolished. The legislators made this recommendation in full knowledge that the state must provide additional funds to local government to replace the lost revenue that abolishing the personal property tax will cause.

In other words, legislative ignorance is much less a political factor than it has been.

Social Policy

The most topical political consideration in the taxation of business today is that which ties tax policy to social policy—the use of taxation to encourage social reform, with revenue generation only a secondary motive.

This is not a new trend in American political history. From time to time in the past we have imposed or abated taxes to settle virgin lands, develop a transportation system, or encourage business development.

But today we are moving into an era when the use of taxation, under political pressure, will have as its primary goal, more than ever before, not revenue yield, but social change. This is the era of "Nader's Raiders," "Give Dirty Water the Works," and "Sue the Polluters."

The Nixon administration has demonstrated a great sensitivity to this aspect of taxation. There are men in the president's administration who are exploring the imposition or abatement of taxes to alleviate our environmental problems—from, for instance, the curtailment of the use of leaded gasoline to the development of recycling programs for waste products.

There are programs under discussion and in the early stages of development to use tax incentives to induce business to take a significant role in the renewal of our inner cities and the training of unskilled workers. I am enthusiastic about some of these developments, apprehensive about others; but as an elected official I cannot ignore the developments that do not please me.

Perhaps that is what it means to be a legislator and sensitive to political considerations. You may be academically 100 percent right in ignoring or condemning a trend in society that may be fiscally disastrous. But if you are an elected official you ignore it at your peril.

There are some who say it is better to be right and not reelected. There are some who say it is better to be reelected than right. There are others—and I count myself among them—who say it is better to be reelected *and* right as often as you can!

15

Political Considerations in the Structure of Local Taxation

Roman S. Gribbs

I particularly welcome the opportunity to speak on this topic of political considerations in the structure of local taxation. With all due respect to the other topics which appear on the program—and to the eminent speakers who present them—I am personally convinced that in any discussion labeled "How Should State and Local Governments Tax Business?" it is the political considerations to which the closest attention must be given.

Political Considerations Paramount

It is the nature of the local tax formulation and implementation process in our nation today that political considerations determine the type and the extent of local taxes on business, virtually to the exclusion of all others. Perhaps this is not as it should be. Perhaps the nation would be better served if nonpolitical considerations were predominant. Even using the word "political" in its broadest and best sense, such considerations may not be the best basis for determining local tax policy as it affects business.

Ideally, such policy ought to reflect the composite views of economists, businessmen, sociologists, tax administrators, and all other affected and interested experts, as well as those of political leaders. Ideally, the recommendations of objective and highly professional organizations such as the Advisory Commission on Intergovernmental Relations ought to be carefully considered in adopting and implementing such policy.

But those of us who have to impose taxes upon business at the local level do not do so under ideal conditions. On the contrary, we face conditions which are both critical in their timing and formidable in their complexity. We act, I am sorry to say, in an atmosphere of near desperation in which nonpolitical considerations seldom intrude.

The Detroit Experience

In Detroit, when I assumed office less than a year ago, we were facing a deficit of some $20 million for the fiscal year then in progress. In addition, we pro-

139

jected a revenue gap of some $49 million during the forthcoming fiscal year. The demand for new services, including badly needed additional police, narcotics programs, and hospital aides could have required still another $50 million.

At the same time, our citizens, including our business firms, were already the most heavily taxed in the state. Our state legislature was understandably reluctant to levy additional taxes or to pass enabling legislation so that Detroit could levy additional taxes. And the law, local and state, limited our options for action most severely. As a newly elected mayor, I was faced with the necessity of formulating and securing approval of a tax program within a matter of a few brief months. Under those conditions, the question of new taxes on local business firms was made within primarily political considerations. It could not have been otherwise.

Specifically, we increased the real estate tax rate and we secured passage of a bill allowing an excise tax on utility bills. Both actions undoubtedly put our own business firms at a disadvantage compared with their out-of-town competitors. Both may have increased the proportionate share of the tax burden on business as opposed to our other taxpayers.

We did not involve economists and businessmen and tax experts in the decision-making process nearly as much as we would have liked. I stand convinced that we did not have the opportunity to do so.

Critical Situation of Local Governments

Detroit is characteristic. The nation's large cities are all in comparable circumstances. They have to have more funds whatever their type or source—not to thrive, but to stave off utter disaster. Many, and perhaps most, smaller cities and many school districts are in equally serious straits. In community after community the order of the day is to curtail all but the most essential services, to postpone new programs, to offer inadequate pay raises to public employees, and to go deeper into debt. Local government, and state government too, is faced with certain disagreeable facts which cannot be refuted.

It is a fact, for example, that while the gross national product has increased by about 84 percent during the past decade, state and local governments have had to more than double their expenditures from $61 billion in 1960 to $127 billion in 1969—and still they have not been able to provide necessary services.

It is a fact that while local government already spends nearly 45 percent of its revenues on education, the quality of educational programs leaves a great deal to be desired and many school districts totter on the brink of bankruptcy.

It is a fact that while local governments bear almost 97 percent of the cost of police protection and correction, they can presently afford to allot no more than 10 percent of their revenues to this essential function despite a spiraling increase in the crime rate. (Parenthetically, Detroit is an exception where approximately 20 percent of our budget is for police protection.)

It is a fact that while local governments are beset with citizen demands for more and better service, they can presently afford to spend only about 20 percent of their revenues for the combined functions of parks and recreation, public welfare programs, sewerage, refuse collection, street cleaning, public buildings, water supply, libraries, housing and urban renewal, airports, parking, and a host of other activities.

How, under these conditions, can the taxation of business be a matter of cool, deliberate, sensible policy formulation? What politicians do is to save their communities—if only temporarily—by grabbing any life preserver they can reach. Long range implications, economic impact, equity, and other considerations must sometimes be put aside in the quest for survival.

Most political leaders whom I know are intelligent and well-informed men. They are dedicated and sincere and honest. They understand, for example, that the imposition of a particular tax on business might drive some firms out of their jurisdictions, with the attendant loss of jobs and other benefits. They know that a tax may be regressive in its effects, that it may be difficult and expensive to collect, that it may be unfair and onerous, and that it may not produce enough additional revenue. But still they enact that tax because it is politically feasible. Politically, the overriding consideration is an immediate need to stay afloat a little while longer.

Thus, my view that political considerations play the major role in determining how state and local governments tax business. Nor do I foresee any immediate prospects of change in this situation.

In public education, the school-age population has grown twice as rapidly as the growth rate of the total population in recent years, and it appears that this will continue. It is on this basis that the Office of Education estimates that the cost of education, which was $16.8 billion in 1955 and $45.1 billion in 1965, will increase to $65.9 billion by 1975. Local governments will have to pick up about half of that increase.

This does not include the additional cost of new school buildings. Here, the estimates of the Office of Education are that the 1965 outlays of $3.7 billion will increase to $5.3 billion by 1975. State-local outlays for publicly supported college buildings will also increase from $1.2 billion in 1965 to $2.5 billion in 1975.

In public safety, the need for more and better-paid, better-trained, and better-equipped police officers must be obvious to all. Only about one-third of the nation's police departments are fully manned at present, and many of this one-third could use more men to great advantage. Salaries must be increased if the kind of men we want and need in police work are to be attracted and retained, for the top salary in half of the nation's departments is less than $7,000. Massive training programs must be developed and implemented, and these are expensive.

The proof of the need is to be seen in the rising incidence of lawlessness and in the understandable fears of the citizens. When I ran for office in Detroit, crime was the number one issue. It still is, and it will be until we can spend what it costs to control it properly.

I realize that the picture I have painted so far is indeed a gloomy one, and it will get worse before it gets better. But let me say at this point that there *is* a solution. There *is* a light at the end of the tunnel. Just bear with me. Put the present situation in its rather dismal perspective. To continue . . .

In public health, we expect government's share of the cost to more than double from 1970 to 1975. Here, the federal government will undoubtedly help, but the burden on local units will still grow substantially. Life expectancy will rise and better health care will be rendered. This will be of unquestioned worth, but it will be very costly.

More hospitals will be needed. The Joint Economic Committee of the United States Congress estimates that state-local outlays for hospitals and other health facilities will increase from $500 million in 1965 to $1.7 billion in 1975. At the same time, the American Hospital Association predicts that the cost of maintaining patients in those hospitals will increase by about 18 percent per year for the next several years.

In public housing, new costs to local government could be astronomical. Low-income families in the United States, according to the Housing Act of 1968, need approximately 600,000 new homes per year during the next decade. Even if local government pays only one-third of this cost, public housing may become our single largest expenditure, exceeding even education.

In urban transportation, we are also faced with prospects of enormous additional costs. The Joint Economic Committee has estimated that state-local expenditures for road construction, which were $7.9 billion in 1965, will rise to $15 billion by 1975. The cost of maintaining these highways and streets will also rise proportionately. Highway safety costs, including traffic control devices, could add another billion annually.

This does not include the cost of mass transit systems—subways, busses, commuter trains, and the like. Nothing is more necessary to the survival of the cities. But who can even guess at the tremendous costs to the cities which may be involved?

I could go on and tabulate further expectations as to increased cost burdens on local units of government. Pollution control and recreation programs and facilities and welfare programs and narcotics control and urban renewal and many others come quickly to mind.

At the same time that these costs will be rising, our revenue producing powers have already reached a point where they cannot reasonably be expected to meet even current needs.

Reaction of Local Political Leaders

This is by no means due to lack of effort on the part of local political leaders. During the decade 1956-1966, for example, state-local taxes were increased by 123 percent, from $26 billion to $58 billion. Few cities or states escaped the escalator of new taxes, more taxes, increased rates. Most found it necessary to revise upward statutory limits that had long seemed to represent absolute limitations.

Much of that increase involved the property tax. Indeed, it is evidence of our inability to apply anything but political considerations that we have been increasing—not decreasing—the burden of this regressive and inflexible tax on our citizens, both proportionately and in actual dollars. In most cases we have reached the limits of the property tax. Constitutionally imposed limitations which cannot easily be changed establish rate and ratio ceilings. Taxpayer rebellion has become obvious through a nationwide experience of rejected millage referenda.

New construction, which should be the basis for new assessments and therefore for new funds from the property tax, has not solved the problem in most cases. In fact, in many cases it has not even kept pace with those factors which reduce the tax rolls, such as demolitions for expressways, deterioration, and tax exemptions.

We have also enacted local sales taxes, income taxes, excise taxes, and a host of nuisance taxes, user charges, fines, and penalties, and made other efforts to increase our revenues. These have produced, in total, only about 15 percent of local government's revenues, leaving us to depend on the real estate tax for the rest. Moreover, they represent a well from which we cannot draw any greater amounts of water and which we can only hope will not go entirely dry. For in some cases we are in competition for these same revenues with the federal or state governments. In others the cost of administration and collection is very high. In others we have pressed taxpayers to the point of open refusal to pay.

I can say with certainty that in Detroit there are no realistic prospects of significantly increasing revenues from these sources. We would help ourselves considerably, for example, if we could get our legislature to allow us to impose a higher income tax on persons who work in but do not reside in the city. But even if this last gasp effort is successful, the added revenues will certainly not bridge the vast gap between income and need.

Nor is borrowing the answer to the problem of meeting the increased costs. The nation's total state-local debt was $15 billion at the end of World War II. It rose to $70 billion at the close of fiscal 1960. It is now over $140 billion. The Joint Economic Committee predicts that it will reach the $200 billion mark in 1975.

I share the view of others that the cities will very soon have exhausted their borrowing capacity, since it must be based not on need, but on ability to repay. Many cities have already exhausted the ability to carry even the current staggering bonded indebtedness with its burdensome interest rates.

It is not my purpose to cast a pall of total gloom on these proceedings. Local government's costs are going up much faster than is our means of meeting them, it is true. This has and will have an adverse effect on business taxation. But I do not detail these present and future costs and revenue problems for the purpose of expressing pessimism.

Instead, it is my purpose to attempt to convince you that you cannot reasonably expect to achieve an adequate local tax program for business under present circumstances. You must first do something which will get political decision makers out of the direct path of onrushing disaster. You must first place cities in a position where political considerations can in fact be coupled with nonpolitical considerations.

To do otherwise is very much like trying to plot a different and more direct course to a ship's destination at the same time that it is sinking. The navigator, in that case, ought to drop his charts and grab his bailing bucket.

I believe that I speak for political leaders at the local level throughout the nation when I say that we have no choice under present crisis circumstances but to get as much revenue from business as we possibly can. Don't talk to us now about the quality of the local tax system or about the policy implications or about the quantitative distribution of the tax burden. Instead, help us first to obtain a way of reducing our need to tax business as unwisely as many of us now do.

Federal Revenue Sharing a Way Out

This is not, in my opinion, an unreasonable request. Fortunately, there is a good, practical way out of our dilemma. (And this is the light at the end of the tunnel about which I spoke earlier.) I refer to the local sharing of income taxes levied by the federal government.

Revenue sharing, in other words, can be the means whereby we at the local level can meet our critical needs without treating business unfairly and inequitably in the process. It is, in my opinion, the only answer to the tax problem of local government and local business alike.

Time restrictions do not permit me to discuss at this time any of the pros and cons of the various revenue sharing proposals which have been suggested. Nor will I discuss the questions of the size of the federal appropriation which should be made for this purpose, the formula for its distribution, the role of the states, or any of the other controversial aspects of revenue sharing. It would also be superfluous for me to recount the arguments in favor of returning taxes levied on individuals to the home communities of those individuals to meet the greatest needs of those individuals.

Suffice it to say that I have no quarrel with those who wish to couple the concept with other progressive steps, such as the reorganization of state governments. I do not disagree with those who want to achieve tax reduction as well as revenue sharing. Least of all do I find fault with those who want to consider revenue sharing in terms of its effect upon inflation and recession and employment and other economic factors.

In the brief time remaining, I want to expand upon my thesis that revenue sharing is the prerequisite of a sound local tax policy for business. Consider, for example, what it would mean if revenue sharing were to be achieved under the Heller plan of 2 percent of the federal individual income tax base. Based on 1970 returns, I estimate that the federal government would have over $7 billion to distribute for meeting local needs.

What a marvelous effect this would have on our state and local governments. What a wonderful opportunity to begin to solve so many of our urban problems. What a wonderful opportunity to begin to restructure our local and state tax policies in keeping with the best interests of society as a whole. What a wonderful opportunity to restore political considerations to their proper niche.

Others in Congress have proposed plans which are similar in many respects to that of Dr. Walter W. Heller—Congressman Henry S. Reuss, Senator Charles E. Goodell, Senator Joseph D. Tydings, and many others. The National Advisory Commission on Urban Problems, chaired by former Senator Paul Douglas, has recommended revenue sharing. The Governors' Conference in 1966 and the National Conference of Mayors and the National League of Cities and the National Association of Counties have expressed their enthusiastic endorsement. Both major political parties—including both presidential candidates in 1968— have supported the concept of revenue sharing, and President Nixon has done so since he took office.

What still seems to be needed is something on the order of massive grassroots support. The public at large apparently still needs to be heard from. Sooner or later that too will happen. Perhaps not until things get even worse in the cities. Perhaps sooner, if Americans are wise enough to grasp solutions as soon as they become evident.

Conclusion

I am sorry that I have not been able to adhere as closely as you may have wished to the topic which was assigned me. Realistically, I could not have done so. It does us no good to delude ourselves. In the vernacular of the times, we must "tell it like it is." The fact is that local tax policy today is not a mix of political and nonpolitical considerations, blended rationally by objective men. To pretend that it is would be wrong.

It is also a fact that local tax policy will not be what we all want it to be until local units of government possess some greater share of the nation's total tax revenues. Until then they cannot afford to give nonpolitical considerations anything resembling the weight to which they are properly entitled.

Perhaps the Tax Institute of America can become a successful instrument for change in restoring to political leaders the opportunity to be less political in developing local tax policy. I would urge you to look at revenue sharing as the first step in the direction of doing so and, in the process, of achieving the ends to which you are dedicated as individuals and as an organization.

16

Discussion of Impact of Political Considerations[a]

Chairman George K. Dunn, *Zenith Radio Corporation*: Mayor Gribbs, we thank you very much for your statement this morning. I don't really consider that that was a major departure from the assigned topic. It seems to me to be right to the point.

Have we any questions or comments with respect to the Mayor's remarks?

Mr. Robert Kleine, *Michigan Budget Division*: I would like to know if the mayor thinks that metropolitan government, such as Jacksonville and Memphis and several other cities have adopted, is any possible solution to the tax situation of the inner cities.

Mayor Roman S. Gribbs, *City of Detroit*: I think the concept is very good. The most successful attempt at metro government is in Toronto. There are a number of other cities which have tried it with varying degrees of success.

Frankly, I fear it is not feasible in Michigan in the near future. As a Michigan citizen, you know of the operations of the Southeast Michigan Council of Governments. This is a voluntary organization which has received considerable criticism and opposition as an infringement upon the authority of smaller units of government.

The metro government approach would bring about the desired end of a consistent tax policy but it will not become politically feasible until there is a tax crisis which will affect every unit of government in the area.

Mr. Leonard E. Kust, *Cadwalader, Wickersham & Taft*: Mayor Gribbs, I assume by your emphasis on revenue sharing, that considering it from the point of view of the politics, the fundamental politics involved, you regard revenue sharing as more attainable than what I would think is an alternative, that is, reassignment of program responsibilities.

If the urban centers were relieved of the high and growing cost of welfare and of school education—shifting education to the state level as Governor Milliken has suggested in Michigan and other people are suggesting, and as some of the CED recommendations provide, and if welfare costs were taken over by the federal government—would that not then very substantially aid in solving the problems of the urban centers? Do you not advocate that because of political considerations?

[a]Since Senator Arrington was a luncheon speaker, and there was no discussion following his address, this chapter relates only to the discussion of the paper by Mayor Gribbs.

Mayor Gribbs: I encourage and support a federal welfare takeover but it is not the final solution to the problems of the cities. For one thing, the benefits in most states would go directly to the state coffers and we would have to depend upon the state legislatures to pass that along to the cities.

All the major cities of America are in the same circumstances as Detroit and I think we can sell the concept of revenue sharing this year.

I might add that Governor Milliken and the state legislature have made a valiant effort on behalf of Detroit in this regard. For the first time in history, the state of Michigan has made a direct, no-strings monetary grant to Detroit in the amount of $5 million. The governor introduced this desperately needed bill and we were able to get it through the legislature this year. It is, I think, a landmark action and is appropriate; and there is no reason, in my judgment, that the federal government cannot do likewise in terms of meeting the needs of the cities, particularly the large cities, the core cities, the old cities, those that are in a crisis situation.

We just can't wait, in the large cities, seven, eight, or ten years for the solution to be found. We in Detroit need money next year starting July 1. The need for increased revenue will approximate $50 million. Our total budget this fiscal year is $580 million. So we need a 10 percent increase next year. We have no place to go.

Statutory limitations prohibit increasing the income tax, property tax, any kind of tax. Barring such increases we must curtail services, and you know what that means in terms of social problems in the large core cities.

Mr. Charles E. Venus, *University of Arkansas*: Mayor, I think your talk was tremendous, and I agree with it. Unfortunately, my congressman happens to be one of the guys blocking what you are talking about.

Mayor Gribbs: Did you reelect him?

Mr. Venus: Wilbur Mills always gets elected.

Mayor Gribbs: At least you know what I talk about when I talk about the political arena.

Mr. Venus: His problem, and we have talked about it—I have talked to him several times about it—is the Ways and Means Committee. It is required to raise the revenue that the federal government spends with practically no control over how it is spent. I wonder if your comment about ground swell from the people is as appropriate as his argument that Congress and the administration simply must realign our national priorities back to where the people are, and he is worried about this kind of control. You can't continue to operate with what looks like what is going to be a $20 billion deficit in the federal budget and not reallocate our national priorities to the national level first. So the problem to me is in the United States Congress.

Mayor Gribbs: I agree, and among those realignments of national priorities is direct help to the cities, the urban areas. This is where we have seen friction over the last four or five years with disturbances and riots stopping short of revolution.

Thus, aid to the cities should be the number one item on the national list of priorities, in my judgment, not because I am Mayor of Detroit, but because Detroit's problems are repeated time and again in almost every urban area throughout the country. Perhaps, as you indicated, the people will become increasingly aware of the urgent social needs in our cities and will demand a solution. That solution will, of course, require considerable additional funds and I need hardly remind you that the federal government is the only agency which has, in effect, an open end on taxation.

Part V:
Revenue Sharing as an
Alternative

17

Decentralizing the Public Sector: Implications for the Business Firm

Murray L. Weidenbaum

In order to gain some insight into the changing relationships between business and government, I find it useful to begin with a view out over the horizon, to the middle of the decade of the 1970s, when we can get a better picture of what the post-Vietnam economic environment will look like.

The United States in Mid-1970s

One basic aspect seems rather assured. The United States will be bigger, much bigger, almost any way that we measure it. The population of the United States will continue to grow, from 205 million at the present time to about 220 million in 1976. And we will be producing more. The gross national product will be growing faster than the population. It almost sounds like an exercise in astronomy. The GNP in 1976 is likely to be about $1.5 trillion. By way of perspective, we should reach the $1 trillion rate early in 1971.

But, will we, as a people, be any better off than we are now? Frankly, this is not a case where bigger necessarily means better. It is conceivable that we could find ourselves devoting a great part of that extra $.5 trillion to cleaning up a rising amount of pollution, to controlling ever-growing problems of crime, or to an escalating arms race.

Sometimes we forget what the statistics are all about. We are not assembled in a great national effort to maximize the GNP. GNP and similar statistics are all attempts to symbolize or serve as a proxy for something more vital—the improved welfare of the American people. In general, it has been true in the past that the more we produced, the more resources were available to deal with the problems facing our society. But we recently have come to realize that the very ways in which we produce and consume can, in themselves, give rise to some of these basic problems.

Therefore, although we cannot with great confidence state that the American economy of 1976 will be a better place than it is today, we can come up with two quite important conclusions: (1) it could be a better place because we will have more resources available to do the things we wish to do, and (2) it certainly will be a different place.

I would like to dwell on those differences for a bit. The first of these differences may well be the shift of emphasis to the private sector, and particularly to the consumer.

Expanding the Consumer Segment

As a nation we are taking important actions which will tend to expand the consumer segment of the American economy in the long run. This is part and parcel of the shift that the Nixon administration is trying to accomplish to a less governmental and to a more private sector orientation in our economy.

I would like to offer just a few numbers for purposes of illustration. Last year consumer spending accounted for 62 percent of the gross national product. This year it may rise to 63 percent. By 1976, perhaps 64 percent of the GNP will be devoted to personal consumption expenditures.

One percent may not sound like much. However, in a trillion-dollar economy, it means about $10 billion more sales to consumers in a twelve-month period. In absolute terms, the magnitudes are quite striking—personal consumption expenditures may rise from $576 billion in 1969 to about $1 trillion in 1976.

In part, of course, this shift in favor of the consumer is coming about as a result of the substantial cutbacks in federal government purchases, particularly for military and space programs. More fundamentally, however, consumer purchasing power is being bolstered through tax relief and reform, as well as by economic growth. The comprehensive tax bill enacted by the Congress late in 1969 contained many important changes in specific tax provisions, ranging from less generous oil depletion allowances to tightening the treatment of capital gains. On balance, however, the act provided for a schedule of substantial tax reductions for individuals. In contrast, the overall tax requirements of corporations were increased.

In the fiscal year 1971, individuals will be paying about $2 billion less federal income tax than they would have if the law had not been passed. With a reasonable pattern of economic growth, the tax savings for individuals will rise to $6 billion in fiscal 1972 and to well over $12 billion in the fiscal year 1976.

These substantial tax reductions will show up in greater consumer purchasing power and in expanding consumer spending, a growth which is likely to be considerably more rapid than for the economy as a whole.

The Public Sector[1]

With this background, I would now like to turn to the future role of the public sector in the American economy. Important changes are likely in the public economy. I anticipate several dominant trends in the public sector of the United States during the coming decade. In view of continuing social tensions, the emphasis on urban problems will probably increase and outlays for people-oriented programs (so-called investments in human capital) will grow. Wider uses will be found for the results of science and new technology in domestic programs. Virtual stability in federal civilian employment will continue, with the continued rises taking place in the work forces of state and local governments, government-oriented corporations, and private nonprofit institutions.

The prospect is for a mixed economy in the United States, but a far more intricate mixture than has been experienced thus far. In the past, most discussions of the role of government have simplistically assumed a clean dividing line between public and private. The very phrase "mixed economy" has mainly indicated that the line was not being drawn at either extreme, that both public and private production occurred in a given industry. For example, the Tennessee Valley Authority and the Pacific Gas and Electric Company both produce and distribute power, the former being a government agency and the latter a private corporation. The Post Office Department and the Railway Express Agency both deliver parcels; again, one is public and the other private.

The mixed economy that is now developing is different. It is characterized by mixed organizations, each of which possesses characteristics of both public institutions and private organizations. The most obvious examples are the large defense contractors and the not-for-profit research laboratories that do most of their business with the federal government.

It appears likely that in coming years increasing proportions of federal funds will be disbursed via mechanisms external to the federal establishment itself—such as state and local governments, intergovernmental agencies, government-oriented corporations, quasi-private institutions, and perhaps even newer organizations possessing both public and private characteristics. The typical federal agency indeed probably will be a policy formulator and overseer of programs dealing with operations which have been decentralized in a variety of ways and over a wide span of the American economy.

Decentralization of Public Sector Programs

There are basic reasons for predicting the greater decentralization of the American public sector. When President Nixon first outlined the principles of his domestic program, he described one of this country's more pressing needs as follows:

If there is one thing we know, it is that the Federal Government cannot solve all the nation's problems by itself; yet, there has been an over-shift of jurisdiction and responsibility to the Federal Government. We must kindle a new partnership between government and people, and among the various levels of government.[2]

The evidence of "over-shift" is readily apparent. Just to catalog the current domestic programs of the federal government now requires a book of more than 600 pages.

In retrospect, it is quite clear that this large flow of power from the private sector and from the cities and states to Washington did not just happen of its own accord. It was induced initially by economic crises. It was further stimulated by mobilization for major war and the threat of major war. It has been accelerated by a variety of efforts of the federal government to cure major domestic ills through the power of federal programs and federal money.

Yet for all this emphasis on the assumed power and influence of our national government, the limits to its effectiveness have become all too apparent. Too often, federal funds have been wasted or used inefficiently. Too often, a bountiful promise has been followed by a lack of performance. Too often, the application of some centrally formulated regulation has failed to accommodate the diversity of local situations. The result has been erosion of public confidence in the federal government's ability to serve as a truly effective instrument of social progress.

State and local governments are often better able to deal with these problems. These governments have also experienced rapid growth. Indeed, since World War II, their expenditures, employment, and indebtedness have increased significantly faster than those of the federal government. Yet the services the public has expected them to provide—education, transportation, health, and many more—have often been beyond the capacity of local public resources to finance and hence to deliver.

The federal government has not been oblivious to the needs of state and local governments. Federal grants-in-aid to states and localities will pass the $27 billion mark this fiscal year, up from $7 billion in 1960. This type of program or categorical assistance has represented an increasing portion of both the federal budget and state and local revenues. But, too often, it has also been accompanied by an ever-growing maze of program restrictions, matching provisions, project approval requirements, and a host and variety of administrative burdens. The result has been the creation of a complicated network of intergovernmental assistance with many inefficiencies.

This administration intends to correct the inefficiencies and inflexibilities of the present system while assisting the states and localities in a more substantial way than in the past.

The challenge, then, is to redesign our system of intergovernmental assistance to achieve the results we all desire:

— a better allocation of total public resources,
— more responsiveness in public institutions,
— more control over local events by local authorities,
— greater program and budget flexibility for locally-elected officials,
— more efficient, less encumbered forms of federal assistance.

The Nixon administration has accepted this challenge. Last year, the president proposed to the Congress fundamental revisions in both the spirit of our intergovernmental relations and in the substance of our intergovernmental assistance system. As he put it, we are seeking to build a "New Federalism," with a return to the states, cities, and counties of the decision-making power rightfully theirs. The "New Federalism" embraces three major sets of actions: improving the basic programs, modernizing management, and decentralizing decision-making in the public sector.

Basic reform of federal programs is being undertaken in such major functional areas as pollution control, welfare, unemployment insurance, and mass transit; legislation to bring about these changes has already made considerable headway in the Congress. A new environmental financing authority is being developed which is designed to ease the pressures on state and local bond markets. The administration has recommended a new long-term program to assist urban transportation, through grants to communities to modernize and expand mass transit facilities and services. We have designed the first fundamental overhaul of the unemployment compensation system since the 1930s. Our family assistance program combines income maintenance with work and training requirements.

Management processes for federal aid and other programs also are being overhauled. This is an area that has long been overdue for attention. The regional boundaries of the major domestic departments of the federal government are being modified so that their headquarter cities are the same and the regions which they cover conform. A new Office of Intergovernmental Relations has been created in the Office of the Vice President.

In order to foster more rational decision making on the whole gamut of domestic programs, President Nixon developed a far-reaching reorganization plan. The plan establishes a new Domestic Affairs Council. All of the Cabinet officers with important responsibilities for domestic programs are on the Council—the secretaries of Health, Education and Welfare, Transportation, Housing and Urban Development, Agriculture, Interior, Labor, Commerce, and Treasury, the attorney general, and the postmaster general.

The Domestic Affairs Council provides a forum for considering all of the various federal activities and functions that affect the states and their subdivisions.

We are attempting to decentralize the public sector in several ways—through revising grant program procedures, through an overhauled manpower training program, and, most strikingly, through the innovation of revenue sharing.

In the grant-in-aid area, the Nixon administration has recommended legislation that would (1) authorize the president to consolidate closely related programs, (2) fund jointly in a single package closely related grant programs within the same federal agency, and (3) authorize joint funding of projects across agency lines.

The manpower training changes are basically intended to encourage the states to take on responsibilities which are now frequently carried out mainly at the federal level.

But perhaps the most innovative aspect of the New Federalism is the proposal for a program of sharing federal revenue with state and local governments. It is the revenue sharing program that he was describing when President Nixon stated in a message to the Congress:

... Ultimately, it is our hope to use this mechanism to so strengthen State and local government that by the end of the coming decade, the political landscape of America will be visibly altered, and States and cities will have a far greater share of power and responsibilities for solving their own problems. . . .[3]

Basically, the revenue sharing proposal federalizes the individual income tax. Specifically, a statutorily determined percentage of the personal tax base will be paid back each year to the states, counties, and cities. There will be no federal controls over the use of the money. We are not only decentralizing the expenditure of public sector funds, but also the decision making on the allocation of these funds. Revenue sharing, in contrast to the specified controls that accompany federal grants-in-aid to state and local governments, would truly be a new departure in our federal form of government.

Although the programs of the New Federalism involve long-term and structural changes, the shift in emphasis can already be seen in the current federal budget. This can be seen most clearly when we examine two separate but related items: (1) the personnel of federal agencies, and (2) financial assistance to state and local governments.

The federal budget for the fiscal year 1971 proposes to continue the reduction in direct federal employment begun last year. From a total of 2,634,000 full-time permanent civilian employees in the executive branch as of June, 1969, we estimate that the total will be down to 2,597,000 by June, 1971.[4]

In contrast, federal financial aid to state and local governments will be rising during this same period, to help our states, cities, and counties to carry out programs of national significance. The estimated total of $27 billion of federal aid to state and local governments in 1971 is an almost fourfold increase since 1961.

Business and the Public Sector

The changing nature of the public sector will have numerous and substantial impacts on private industry, particularly on the various companies that either do business with the government or are regulated by it, and also on those that merely look at government as a source of competition or interference. In any of these regards, I believe that it is necessary to understand the potential impacts of these future developments.

The traditional discussion of the public sector brings to mind images of thousands and thousands of clerks working in innumerable bureaus and agencies who, on occasion, purchase pens, pencils, paper, desks, and chairs from private firms.

Let us face it, this idyllic picture of the public sector does not conform to the realities of the twentieth century, if indeed it ever did earlier. The civil service clerk preparing innocuous reports that are to be duplicated, filed, and refiled, although a stock figure of dramatic fiction, represents a trivial case of public resource utilization.

When viewed as a whole, the modern public sector, as it has developed in the United States, is characterized by four basic changes:

1. A widespread reliance upon government-oriented corporations and other quasi-private organizations that perform government functions under close surveillance;
2. A massive use of advanced research concepts and high technology;
3. Shifting relationships between federal and state governments, with more of the funds coming from the federal treasury, but more of the end activities being performed by states and their subdivisions; and
4. Government expansion into areas for which traditional public agencies are not well equipped but in which private markets may not yet exist to any significant degree.

The changing institutional structure of the public sector will have important repercussions on the location of government customers and the nature of sales to them by private industry. The growing decentralization of government activities will mean that federal agencies based in Washington will award a declining proportion of government contracts. More public sector contracts will come from the agencies of fifty state governments and from thousands of local jurisdictions, often using funds received from the federal government.

At present, much of the state and local government market is in the hands of local firms. Greater opportunities will develop in the coming decade for aggressive national corporations that can learn to deal effectively with the multitude of local purchasing agents and procurement codes. Moreover, as states and localities shift their purchases to goods and services needed to eliminate poverty and to control environmental pollution, and for other "new" requirements, opportunities will arise for companies which have not traditionally catered to these public sector markets.

To the extent that specialized government contractors, such as government-oriented corporations and private nonprofit organizations, obtain large shares of prime contracts from these governments, the more commercially oriented companies may begin to look to them as fruitful sources of government work via subcontracting. Indeed, a specialization of labor may at times develop. For example, the systems analysis and development work—such as retraining the hard-core unemployed or rebuilding slums—may be awarded in good measure to nonindustrial contractors. Companies experienced in the more traditional fields, however, may continue to perform the construction and standard manufacturing portions of the work, often as subcontractors.

In many cases, the decentralization of federal functions, particularly those involving newer types of goods and services, will provide major opportunities for diversification of markets and product lines to companies alert to these developments and geared to adjusting to the changes required. Some industries may penetrate these emerging public sector markets through internal product development. Typically, these will be firms with strong engineering and systems development capabilities, such as in aerospace, electronics, instrumentation, and ordinance. Thus far, government-oriented companies have not played an important role in domestic welfare or other civilian sector programs. But there are growing pressures to utilize their unique research and development and system management capabilities in these expanding programs. Defense cutbacks have already spurred some military and aerospace companies to seek out cost-plus contracts awarded by civilian agencies; further cutbacks would lead to a redoubling of such efforts. Even now they are increasing in volume.

Many corporations have been setting up new divisions or subsidiaries geared to providing products or systems to public sector customers. Recent organizational changes along these lines have followed one of two paths. Some companies are setting up divisions which focus on one specific public sector market, such as abatement of environmental pollution. Other firms have set up units with broader charters to seek out government business generally. Such company activities can obtain useful guidance for market research and planning by examining the changing priorities of federal government expenditures, along the lines that I discussed earlier.

Some Concluding Observations

In a fundamental but favorable sense, business and government are broadly competitive—in terms of both clientele and money. To the extent that business is responsive to changing public and private needs, there will be lessened pressures for government agencies to step in, either to set national standards or to perform the actual provision of goods and services. The reverse is surely true. To the extent that business is unresponsive, the public sector is likely to grow at the expense of the private sector.

As a nation, we will have very considerable discretion over the use of the tremendous amount of resources that will be available to us during the years that follow the end of the Vietnam War. These resources, in effect, will also come with a challenge, that we use them wisely. If we do not, we may find that economic growth, rather than being translated into improved well-being, may be devoted increasingly merely to ameliorating continuing physical and social ills. This may be the essence of our concern to shift national priorities—to make the necessary investments now in improving the quality of our physical and social environment to permit real improvement in our national welfare in the years to come.

Let me close with a personal forecast. In 1976, the United States will look toward the future with greater confidence than it does today. I say that not because we will have solved our major problems, but because we will have grown more accustomed to dealing at the national level with these difficult questions of social relations, environmental quality, and urban living. The eight years of the Nixon administration—as I said, this is a personal forecast—will not have brought the millennium but they will have provided the framework within which the American people can make substantial progress in a peacetime world.

Notes

1. This material is drawn from my recent book, *The Modern Public Sector* (New York: Basic Books, Inc., 1969).
2. Message to Congress, April 14, 1969.
3. *The New Federalism*, An Address and Statements by President Richard M. Nixon (Washington: Government Printing Office, 1969), p. 51.
4. *The Budget of the United States Government, Fiscal Year 1971* (Washington: Government Printing Office, 1970), p. 550.

**Part VI:
Presidential Address**

18

How Should State and Local Governments Tax Business? The Impact of Institutional Failure

L.E. Kust

Our symposium subject—"How Should State and Local Governments Tax Business?"—is being intensively explored in microcosm from a variety of points of view in our scheduled program. I should like to explore the question from a more general point of view by considering the implications of its institutional context.

As Disraeli observed, it is institutions alone that create a nation. Had he lived in less buoyant and optimistic times he might have gone on to note that it is a failure of institutions that poses for organized society its gravest problems. Unlike the latter half of the nineteenth century, we live in such times.

There are no doubt far graver problems of institutional failure than the problems of how state and local governments should tax business, but I would like to suggest that some of the main problems involved in this question are created by institutional inadequacies.

The Institutional Framework

The institutional framework for our problem is first of all a quantitative one. There are 50 states, 3,070 counties, 403 cities over 50,000 population, and thousands of boroughs, townships, villages, and school districts to take into account when one asks the question how state and local government should tax business. The sheer numbers boggle the mind if, for instance, each of these jurisdictions should impose a tax on the net income of a nationwide business.

This, of course, poses the problem in its most extreme form. But how far back, if at all, do we need to recede from this extreme before the problem of proliferation of taxes on business assumes acceptable proportions? By what means would we impose appropriate restraints?

There is no question that resort by local governments to taxes on business, particularly in the form of direct income taxes and the obligation to collect or pay sales and use taxes, is growing apace.

The first local income tax on corporations was enacted by Toledo, Ohio, in 1946. By 1964 local income taxes on corporations had increased to 95, mostly in Ohio. Now there are 341, still mostly in Ohio (300), but also in Kentucky (23), Michigan (13), Missouri (2), Oregon (1), Pennsylvania (1) and New York (1).

165

The first local sales taxes were adopted before World War II by New York City (1934), New Orleans (1936), and Philadelphia (1938, later lapsed). By 1963 thirteen states had authorized local governments to levy sales taxes and by the end of 1964 the number of local governments levying sales taxes had increased to 2,329. There are now twenty-four states that authorize local sales taxes and the number of such taxes now exceeds 3,400.

The imposition of local income or sales-use taxes may not present serious problems in the case of local business, but in the case of nationwide or multistate businesses the proliferation of such taxes, particularly the collection of use taxes, is creating an intolerable compliance and enforcement burden. The Willis Subcommittee on State Taxation of Interstate Commerce examined the impact of local income and sales and use taxes and concluded in 1964 that if the trend then visible continued, the compliance demands placed by such taxes on interstate business would become as unreal as the local governments' ability to enforce them.[1]

Specifically with respect to local corporate income taxes the Subcommittee concluded that "any significant increase in the number of taxing localities will result in either the substantial expense of filing large numbers of low-liability returns or what is more likely, widespread noncompliance."[2] With respect to local sales and use taxes the Subcommittee observed that "the sheer problem of maintaining separate records of sales for so many localities would be overwhelming to many interstate sellers."[3]

The trend of adoption of such taxes has accelerated since 1964 and the compliance burdens encountered by a large nationwide business such as I was associated with have abundantly substantiated what was anticipated by the Willis Subcommittee.

The Institutional Failures

What is giving growing impetus to these local taxes on business? It is not, I am convinced, a new era of public finance based on higher wisdom. It is instead the consequence of institutional failures which can be summed up in an elegant paradox: Taxation—Too much is not enough.

Clearly, this is the political dilemma of the day; the electorate is rebelling against higher taxes and yet public services are being starved to the dissatisfaction of the same electorate. Someone has observed that when self-interest and duty coincide virtue comes easily. Virtue is unlikely to issue easily out of the present fiscal dilemma.

What is one to make of the irreconcilable public attitudes of tax revolt and demand for more and better public services? Are they merely the product of unthinking irrationality and unbridled self-interest? Or are they the consequence of justifiable frustration with malfunctioning private and public organization resulting in a persistent and intractable mismatching of resources and needs? Perhaps this is only another illustration of the human condition about which Marshall McLuhan has quipped: "Man's reach must exceed his grasp or what's a metaphor?" If you didn't understand that you may share Mort Sahl's sentiment that McLuhan is not meant to be understood, he is meant to be respected.

There is unquestionably a mood of tax revolt in the country today. One reads of schools closed for lack of funds. State legislatures and city councils are rent by bitter disputes over the raising of revenues. There is a prevailing belief that taxes have grown oppressively and simply bear too heavily on family resources diluted by inflation.

Total taxes—federal, state and local—were 25.1 percent of gross national product in 1968. Perhaps this is too high, but they were 24.8 percent of GNP in 1944, 24.9 percent in 1954 and 25.2 percent in 1960. Thus, as a percentage of our economic output, taxes remained virtually constant for a quarter of a century, covering the mature taxpaying life of most of us.

If we decompose the global figures we find that over this period federal taxes declined from 20.6 percent to 17 percent while state and local taxes increased from 4.8 percent to 8.1 percent, keeping the total essentially constant as already indicated. But here we begin to find the foundation of our dilemma.

Taxes have given the appearance of rising prodigiously. We all conveniently forget that federal taxes have been reduced twice since the Korean War, by an average of 20 percent the last time in 1964 and 1965. On the other hand, we vividly remember the increases in rates and the new taxes at the state and local level. The fact that the federal reductions and the state and local increases have essentially balanced is lost on most of us and the shift in tax burdens from the federal to the state and local level has given an appearance of rising taxes. On top of this the 10 percent federal surcharge together with social security and state and local tax increases added substance to the appearance. In 1969 total taxes increased to 28 percent of GNP, from 25.1 percent in 1968, accounted for mostly by the federal surcharge. With the repeal of the federal surcharge there will be a decline in the federal burden, but the repeal of the surcharge, together with additional federal tax reductions provided by the Tax Reform Act of 1969, will I am sure again be unavailing to change the public attitude toward increased state and local taxes.

The appearance of rising taxes is more apparent than real not only because of the shift between federal and state and local tax burdens, but also because state and local tax structures are relatively sluggish in their response to economic growth and, therefore, new taxes and rate increases are required more frequently than with a more elastic tax structure.

A progressive personal income tax such as at the federal level will without any change in rates produce revenue growth greater than economic growth—the so-called fiscal dividend. Hence, the federal government reaps an increase in revenues to finance new needs without legislation to increase rates and there is no appearance of rising taxes.

On the other hand, the property taxes which provide 86 percent of local tax revenues and about 42 percent of state and local tax revenues barely grow with rising income and provide no "fiscal dividend."

While other elements of state and local tax structures, such as a sales tax and, of course, a personal income tax, are more responsive to economic growth, the overall relative inelasticity of state and local tax structures has required recurring increases in assessments or rates and the addition of new taxes as the revenue burden has shifted from the federal level to the state and local level.

Although taxes may have given the appearance of having risen too high, are present revenues sufficient? I think clearly they are not. The cost of social overheads must inevitably rise in an increasingly urbanized and industrialized society. As Mr. Justice Holmes has wisely observed, taxes are the cost of civilized society. Civilization is preeminently an urban phenomenon.

The governmental services expected and unavoidably required by an urban society call, it seems to me, for an increasing allocation of the gross national product to the governmental sector.

If one considers the greater impact of inflation on the public sector than on the private sector because of the inability in the public sector effectively to offset inflation with productivity gains through new technology as in the private sector, there should, merely to maintain the same level of public services, have been a shift upward in the required revenues in relation to GNP. Instead, revenues have remained essentially constant in relation to GNP.

Shifts in the relative burden of national defense expenditures and shifts between federal and state and local expenditures obscure and complicate a quantitative analysis, but the pressure for more public revenues to cover demonstrable needs, for example, with regard to education, crime controls, pollution, traffic and transportation, are quite sufficient in themselves to persuade the informed that existing revenue structures are not adequate.

We can, of course, hope, and perhaps expect if proper policies are pursued, that the private sector can increasingly provide the social overhead needs of an urban society without the direct intervention of government. This, rather than a growing governmental sector, would better keep faith with the traditional American disposition toward an open, pluralistic, autonomous, and relatively unstructured society. This also might better engage the energies and convictions of our troubled young generation.

But in the absence of effective means of private sector response to the needs the governmental sector has carried the burden.

It is in this context of intensifying taxpayer revolt and growing governmental burdens that a failure of institutional response has led to questionable proliferation of local taxes on business.

The details may vary from state to state but the pattern is familiar and repeats itself with disquieting similarity. The resistance to additional taxes, the conflicts between rural and urban legislators, the conflicts between central city and suburbs in metropolitan areas, and an endless supply of transient political quarrels render state legislatures impotent to deal forthrightly with programing and funding the growing demands on government. Lacking state support, local governments, particularly the cities, demand enlarged taxing powers and state legislatures yield to their demand rather than levy additional taxes at the state level.

This in itself might well be desirable except that local governments find their constituents no more receptive to new taxes than do the state legislatures. Taxpayer resistance and the limited ability of central cities to tax suburban residents leads inevitably to the extension of new local taxes on business.

Thus, an inexorable institutional malfunctioning leads to proliferation of local taxes on business. I do not believe that this trend can be permitted to develop to its logical conclusion without an overwhelming compliance burden for nationwide and multistate business.

Toward Solutions—Institutional Reforms

How shall the pressing governmental needs, particularly urban needs, be met without additional local taxes on business?

We have seen that the tax revolt and the revenue crisis are largely the consequence of rigid state and local tax structures that are inadequately responsive to economic growth. The federal tax structure, on the other hand, has permitted reduction in rates while at the same time providing growing revenues to fund new programs.

We have become increasingly aware of this "fiscal mismatch"—the federal government having the tax resources and the state and local governments having the problems.

Two solutions immediately suggest themselves. We can let the federal government assume fiscal responsibility for the problems. Or, accompanied by federal tax reduction, we can revise state and local tax structures to yield the necessary revenues and provide the needed revenue growth in response to economic growth. Federal fiscal responsibility can take the form of direct federal programs, or increases in grants-in-aid, or revenue sharing such as proposed by the administration, or a credit of state and local taxes against the federal income tax.

Federal Revenue Sharing

Enlarged federal programs would perhaps provide a more uniform effort toward solution of the problems suited to the need across the country. But the temper of the times, and rightly so in my judgment, is against more and larger federal programs. The success of existing federally managed programs in many cases leaves much to be desired. Moreover, dependence on federal programs would reverse the slow decentralization of governmental services implicit in the shift in revenues from the federal to the state and local level which most of us applaud as a more agreeable structure of social organization. Thus, new federal programs are not an attractive prospect.

Grants-in-aid have grown faster than any other sector of the federal budget in recent years. They are useful and appropriate in some circumstances. But they have multiplied incredibly and work unevenly, in part because state and local governments often lack the expertise to take advantage properly of all the available grant-in-aid programs.

Revenue sharing has been given growing attention since it was first advocated by Walter W. Heller, former Chairman of the Council of Economic Advisers in the Kennedy and Johnson administrations, to whom, by the way, Congressman John W. Byrnes replied when chided by him for undue devotion to the Puritan ethic in fiscal matters: "Well, I'd rather be a Puritan than a Heller."

Revenue sharing was recommended in the Report to the President and the Congress in December, 1968, by the National Commission on Urban Problems, and has now received official endorsement from the Nixon administration, with a modest beginning. Under the formulas to be applied if the proposal is adopted, it is estimated that when fully effective in the fiscal year 1976 the system will yield $5 billion for sharing with states and local governments. This is unquestionably a more appealing prospect than the first two alternatives considered. But it is subject to grave misgivings about the political wisdom of separating at the state and local level the responsibility for raising revenues from the power to spend revenues. We have all seen some of the capricious consequences of such a separation of responsibility and authority in connection with state aid to local governments. Some of this as employed at the state level may be necessary and tolerable if social overhead needs are to be met and revenue resources are to be equalized. But I have deep reservations about uncritically embracing the principle of revenue sharing at the federal level.

There is an alternative to federal sharing which serves to divert federal revenues to state and local governments without fully relieving these governments from responsibility for raising the revenues. This is the device of a partial credit of state and local taxes against the federal income tax. A number of notable authorities espouse this approach, perhaps the most prestigious of which is the Committee on Economic Development.

Restructuring State and Local
Governments

While some kind of diversion of federal revenues is probably unavoidable in view of the incapacity of present state and local structures to raise the necessary revenues, it would be unfortunate for the future vigor and independence of state and local governments if reliance on federal revenues should delay and divert effort from modernizing state and local governmental structures. I would hope that use of federal revenues for state and local purposes, if they are to be so used, would serve only to tide us over the transitional period during which state and local governments restructure themselves and their tax systems and during which there is some reallocation of program responsibility among the several levels of government.

Restructuring state and local governments and tax systems, however, confronts formidable obstacles, particularly at the local level.

At the state level the primary requirement is to place greater reliance on the personal income tax. The proposal of the Committee on Economic Development would induce this by allowing a credit against the federal tax of only a state personal income tax and not other taxes. The Advisory Commission on Intergovernmental Relations recommends that a modern and responsive state tax structure should rely mainly on two broad-based taxes, the sales tax and the personal income tax.

With respect to local government, the problems are formidable indeed. Not only are there the political obstacles encountered at the state level to changing tax systems; there are also the far more obstinate political obstacles to changing governmental structures. But before modern tax systems can be implemented at the local level municipal taxing powers must be enlarged and municipal boundaries redefined. The National Commission on Urban Problems urges the restructuring of local governments into viable metropolitan areas. A major effort is underway in Minneapolis-St. Paul toward regionalization of the public finance system.

Beyond this we must seek solutions through more imaginative sharing of fiscal responsibility among urban governments, the states, and the federal government. We should not shrink from objectively evaluating the merits of such challenging new approaches as the proposal in Michigan to have the state assume fiscal responsibility for all educational costs, or the proposal of Governor Nelson A. Rockefeller of New York that the federal government assume all welfare costs. It may well be that such a reallocation of responsibilities is not only desirable but necessary to free local resources to meet the new and growing urban problems which can be better met directly at the local level.

The younger generation is challenging all of our established structures. We should accept this challenge, especially where we can ourselves clearly see the deficiencies. Our growing urban society is undeniably presenting us with urgent problems which the old structures are ill-adapted to meet and which we should be prepared to change. Among these are clearly, in my judgment, our rigid state and local tax systems, our antiquated local governmental structures, and the accustomed allocation of fiscal responsibilities among the federal, state, and local governments.

With institutional reforms of the kind suggested the pressure for new local taxes on business should recede. If program responsibilities are properly assigned, local revenue needs could be met through the traditional reliance on the property tax and licenses and through more imaginative and widespread imposition of user charges. If such revenues remain insufficient to meet the costs of services that must be funded locally, then local personal income taxes should be imposed. If sales taxes are used they should apply only to local sales without imposing the obligation on a nonlocal seller to collect a compensating use tax.

Limitation of Local Powers to Tax
Interstate Commerce

In order to hasten the required institutional reforms, Congress should—under its power to regulate interstate commerce—limit the power of local governments to impose on interstate business an income tax or the obligation to collect use tax on interstate sales. There is growing concern that Congress should act more resolutely with respect to the powers of local governments to tax interstate business than with respect to state powers. Federal legislation to define such powers and set uniform standards and the Multistate Tax Compact to administer these standards and to provide continuing surveillance and study of the problems should be encouraged. The proposal of the Ad Hoc Committee on Taxation of Interstate Business advocates such a structure under the commerce and compact clauses of the Constitution.

All of this is not to suggest that interstate business should escape an appropriate share of the state and local tax burden. But because of the compliance and enforcement burdens involved the business share by way of income taxes and collection of use taxes should be met through state level taxes. At the local level the business share should be met through real property taxes, user charges, and licenses with respect to which compliance and enforcement are manageable. An appropriate exception might be made for large city or metropolitan area governments, say over one million in population, where the needs are the greatest. The limited number and the size of such jurisdictions might well make broader local power to tax business acceptable.

Conclusion

A year ago our esteemed past president, Victor Ferrall, eloquently deplored the burgeoning "tax industry." He developed with wisdom and insight the argument that so much talent and effort as is devoted to this "industry" can scarcely be justified. While the thorny economic, political, enforcement, and compliance problems involved in distributing the costs of a growing public sector unavoidably consume more talent and effort than in a simpler past, we should surely strive to minimize such an essentially unproductive use of resources. I would hope that my remarks tonight may help to serve this end.

Notes

1. United States Congress, House of Representatives, Committee on the Judiciary, Special Subcommittee on State Taxation of Interstate Commerce, *State Taxation of Interstate Commerce*, H.R. Report No. 1480, 88th Congress, 2d Session (Washington: Government Printing Office, 1964), pp. 441-80; H.R. Report No. 565, 89th Congress, 1st Session (Washington: Government Printing Office, 1965), pp. 837-74.

2. Ibid., p. 478.

3. Ibid., p. 1187.

About the Contributors

John Shannon is Assistant Director, Taxation and Finance, of the Advisory Commission on Intergovernmental Relations, and has coordinated the preparation of a number of the Commission's reports.

J.E. Luckett is the Director of Finance of Lexington, Kentucky. At the time of the symposium, Mr. Luckett was the Kentucky State Commissioner of Revenue, a position he held for fourteen years.

F.J. Siska, Jr., is the National Manager of State and Local Taxes for Sears, Roebuck and Co., a position to which he was appointed in 1963.

Frederick D. Stocker is Professor of Business Research, Economics and Public Administration at The Ohio State University. Professor Stocker was formerly an economist with the United States Department of Agriculture. He has written extensively on taxation and government finance, especially at the state and local level.

John F. Due is Professor of Economics at the University of Illinois, Urbana. Professor Due's most recent publications are *State and Local Sales Taxation* and *Indirect Taxation in Developing Economies.*

John W. Ingram is the Director of the State Division of the Pennsylvania Economy League, Inc. Mr. Ingram was on leave from that position in 1963-1966 to serve as Secretary of Administration of the Commonwealth of Pennsylvania.

Allen D. Manvel is a consultant on governmental finances and statistics in Washington, D.C. Mr. Manvel was serving as a consultant to the Advisory Commission on Intergovernmental Relations at the time of the symposium.

George F. Break is Professor of Economics and Chairman of the Department of Economics at the University of California, Berkeley. Professor Break is the author of *Agenda for Local Tax Reform*, among other publications.

Lee Hill is General Tax Counsel of the Humble Oil & Refining Company. Mr. Hill serves on the Taxation Committees of the National Association of Manufacturers and the Chamber of Commerce of the United States, among many professional affiliations.

Robert F. Steadman is Director of the Committee for Improvement of Management in Government of the Committee for Economic Development. Mr. Steadman was the chief staff officer for CED in the preparation of a series of policy statements, including *Modernizing Local Government* and *Modernizing State Government*.

W. Russell Arrington has been a member of the Illinois State Senate since 1954, and is Senate Republican Leader. At the time of the symposium, Senator Arrington was President Pro Tempore of the Senate. The Senator is also a member of the Advisory Commission on Intergovernmental Relations.

Roman S. Gribbs has been the Mayor of Detroit since January, 1970. Mayor Gribbs is Vice President of the National League of Cities, Chairman of the Michigan Conference of Mayors, and a member of the Board of Trustees of the United States Conference of Mayors.

Murray L. Weidenbaum holds the Edward Mallinckrodt Distinguished University Professorship at Washington University, St. Louis. At the time of the symposium, he was Assistant Secretary of the Teeasury for Economic Policy and in charge of the development of the Nixon administration's revenue sharing program. Dr. Weidenbaum is the author of *The Modern Public Sector* and numerous articles and papers on government finance.

L.E. Kust is senior tax partner in the New York law firm of Cadwalader, Wickersham & Taft, and was previously vice president and general tax counsel of the Westinghouse Electric Corporation. Mr. Kust served as president of the Tax Institute of America in 1970.